# The War of 1812

Produced by the
Northeast Regional Office
National Park Service

U.S. Department of the Interior
Washington, D.C.

# A Message from the Director

In August 1814, as an invading British army approached the American capital, first lady Dolley Madison instructed her staff to collect valuables from the White House. Among the precious articles saved by the staff was Gilbert Stuart's famous portrait of George Washington. In a collective act of patriotism, they removed the painting from its frame and hid it safely away. The enemy arrived soon after, torched the Capitol and White House, and then turned their sights on Baltimore.

The War of 1812 is often remembered as America's second war of independence, the conflict that produced an enduring symbol of national unity in "The Star-Spangled Banner." While it is one of our lesser-known wars, its repercussions were profound. Though it was fought 200 years ago, the war raises questions that resonate now, questions of national interests, economics, and foreign policy, even civil rights. As steward of America's special places, the National Park Service preserves sites from the War of 1812 and commemorates the story for all generations. Like many of our national parks, those from the War of 1812 offer insight not only into where we've been as a nation, but where we are today. That is the special power of our national parks: The power of place.

This handbook serves as an introduction to a dramatic time when the young republic, outraged over Britain's interference with maritime trade and threats to American citizens at sea, declared war. When the war began, the Americans marched into British Canada for what Thomas Jefferson thought was going to be a simple matter of driving the English off the continent. But it wasn't as easy as that, and the United States found itself caught up in a much broader conflict. By the time British troops marched on the White House in 1814, a dispirited and nearly bankrupt America was negotiating for peace. But fortunes turned on the battlefield, and Americans repulsed British invasions of New York and Baltimore later that year.

In 1815, though the conflict ended in a draw, the United States emerged with a stronger sense of national identity and renewed confidence. Washington's portrait was returned to the White House after the war and hangs in the East Room today, a proud symbol of our national resolve to endure and prosper as well as a tangible connection to the past. That is what makes our national parks such powerful sources of inquiry, understanding, and self-discovery.

The National Park Service is proud to be the steward of these special places that have been set aside for all time by the American people. I hope that this handbook heightens your appreciation of our rich heritage and deepens your personal connection with our collective past.

*Jonathan B. Jarvis*
*Director, National Park Service*

# Table of Contents

*What does it mean to be American?*
*Will our democratic experiment survive?*

# PREFACE

In the midst of a second war of independence, Americans pondered fundamental questions of national identity and destiny that reverberate from 1812 into the conversations at many National Park Service sites. Today, Americans are familiar with iconic symbols forged during the War of 1812: the Defense of Baltimore that sparked the creation of our national anthem, the burning of the White House and Capitol, the Battle of New Orleans, and the exploits of USS *Constitution* (Old Ironsides). Yet, most Americans are unaware that the war's internal and external conflicts continue to shape our national identity.

The War of 1812 involved a wide range of people who fought for vastly different goals. American Indians saw the struggle as one of cultural survival and potential to roll back European expansion. British subjects saw the conflict as a defensive war to prevent the United States from conquering Canada. As in other wars, Americans were divided. Some saw it as an ill-conceived land grab and others viewed it as a necessary action to protect American rights and fulfill the legacy of the Revolution.

The bicentennial of the War of 1812 provides an opportunity for the National Park Service to join Americans and our neighbors in reexamining and connecting with the stories and people of this fascinating, neglected, and misunderstood conflict that firmly established our republic. In this collection of essays, the National Park Service has united with Parks Canada and scholars to share stories about the participants, motives, actions, causes, and consequences of the war.

Alan Taylor's introductory essay sets the stage for what historians have called the "forgotten war," situating the War of 1812 in the "prolonged drama" of the

**On September 14, 1814, Francis Scott Key exultantly witnessed the American flag flying over Fort McHenry, and celebrated the Star-Spangled Banner's survival of the British attack on Baltimore in the lyrics of the song that would become the US national anthem.**

American Revolution. His essay reminds us that the survival of the new nation remained uncertain. The British were convinced that the fledgling republic would fail while many Americans believed that the Canadians would welcome them with open arms. Taking the long view, Donald Hickey and Kathryn Braund demonstrate that war was a byproduct of larger conflicts that raged across Europe and North America for more than a century. The complex allegiances between and among Europeans, European Americans, and Native peoples during the War of 1812 reflected high stakes in the political, economic, cultural, and environmental global contest between Britain and France.

In the decades after the Revolutionary War, America's natural and social landscape experienced profound changes. In turn, altered homelands and boundaries transformed the identities of all North American peoples—African, European, or Native in origin. Andrew Burstein and Nancy Isenberg explore the evolution of the political culture of the early American republic, revealing the partisanship and competing ideologies that charged "Mr. Madison's war" with domestic and foreign rivalries. In their investigations of naval and land operations, Paul Gilje and David and Jeanne Heidler demonstrate that the war was no mere clash of technologies, but a contest of identity and ideology. Gene Smith reminds us that African Americans' pursuit of freedom and equality remained unfulfilled at war's end.

The War of 1812 meant many things to many peoples, and its memory proved even more malleable: Matthew Dennis, Donald Graves, and Doug Kiel examine the war in the collective memories of American, Canadian, and Native nations, exploring the narratives, myths, and symbols that sustain communities and their versions of the War of 1812 through 200 years of history. These reflections on the war's legacy help us to see ourselves in the landscape of history, and invest our experiences in America's national parks—places that provide a palpable connection to the past—with creative and incisive acts of remembering.

# TIMELINE

The War of 1812 was part of a broad conflict between Great Britain and France that embroiled many nations, both European and Native, over the course of a century. From the American perspective the conflict was the final act of the American Revolution. American aspirations to sustain the new republic on a continental scale ultimately brought them into conflict again with their former colonizer, and also with Native nations whose lives, lands, and liberties were threatened in the North American contest between the British Empire and the United States.

In the early 1800s the US Capitol, like the American republic, was a work in progress.

# The Road to War

**October 7, 1763**
Great Britain bars European settlement west of the Appalachian Mountains to limit encroachment on Native lands

**September 3, 1783**
American Revolutionary War ends; Britain's Native allies are left out of the settlement

**July 13, 1787**
US creates Northwest Territory, promising "utmost good faith" towards Indian lands, property, rights, and liberty

**June 19, 1791**
British North America split into Upper Canada (Ontario) and Lower Canada (Quebec)

**February 1, 1793**
France declares war on Great Britain

**November 19, 1794**
Great Britain agrees to withdraw from border forts and to settle Canada's border with the US by commission under terms of Jay Treaty

**1798–1801**
US and France embroiled in Quasi-War

**March 4, 1801**
President Thomas Jefferson inaugurated in Washington, DC

**May 17, 1803**
Napoleonic Wars begin

**May 18, 1804**
Napoleon becomes Emperor of France

**May 22, 1805**
Great Britain issues *Essex* decision, threatening US re-export trade

**April 18, 1806**
US adopts (but suspends) partial nonimportation law against Great Britain

**May 16, 1806**
Great Britain issues first of a series of Orders-in-Council, curtailing American trade with Europe

**November 21, 1806**
France declares retaliatory blockade of Great Britain

**December 31, 1806**
US and Great Britain reach trade agreements in Monroe-Pinkney Treaty

**March 3, 1807**
US repudiates Monroe-Pinkney Treaty without formal agreement on impressment of sailors

**June 22, 1807**
Impressment of three American sailors in *Chesapeake-Leopard* affair sparks US calls for war

**October 17, 1807**
Great Britain limits impressment to British seamen found on neutral merchant vessels

**December 14, 1807**
US initiates trade restrictions against Great Britain

**April 17, 1808**
France begins seizing all American ships entering French ports

**March 1, 1809**
US restricts all trade with Great Britain and France

**March 4, 1809**
President James Madison inaugurated in Washington, DC

**September 30, 1809**
US and select Native chiefs in the Old Northwest agree to cession of 3 million acres in Treaty of Fort Wayne; many Native leaders, including Tecumseh, refuse to recognize the agreement

**March–October 1810**
France issues series of decrees restricting US ships entering French-controlled ports

**October 9, 1811**
Isaac Brock appointed president and administrator of Upper Canada (Ontario)

**October 21, 1811**
George Prevost appointed captain-general and governor-in-chief of Canada

**November 7, 1811**
Battle of Tippecanoe, Indiana Territory

**November 8, 1811**
US burns Prophet's Town, Indiana Territory

# 1812 THE US DECLARES WAR...

**April 4 & 14**
US temporarily bans US ships from leaving port and all exports

**June 1**
US Army departs from Dayton, Ohio for Fort Detroit, Michigan Territory

**June 1**
President Madison sends war message to Congress, initiating first declaration of war under US Constitution

**June 4**
US House of Representatives adopts war bill

**June 8**
US signs treaty with Wyandots, Shawnees, and Mingoes at Urbana securing right to build road through Native lands

**June 17**
US Senate adopts war bill

**Former US Senator Alexander Contee Hanson was seriously injured when a mob attacked his newspaper office during the Baltimore riots.**

**June 18**
War of 1812 begins when President Madison signs war bill into law

**June 22–August 5**
Partisan riots in Baltimore, Maryland

**June 23**
Great Britain repeals Orders-in-Council just days after US declaration of war; news of this concession reaches US in August

**July 12**
US invades Canada across Detroit River

**July 17**
Great Britain captures Fort Mackinac, Michigan Territory

**August 7**
US withdraws from Canada across Detroit River

**August 9**
US and British commanders implement unauthorized Dearborn-Prevost armistice

**August 13**
US captures first British ship during the war when HM Sloop *Alert* surrenders to US Frigate *Essex* in North Atlantic

**August 15**
British-allied Potawatomi and Winnebago warriors attack Fort Dearborn, Illinois Territory

**August 16**
Great Britain captures Detroit, Michigan Territory

**August 19**
USS *Constitution* defeats HMS *Guerriere* in North Atlantic, earning nickname "Old Ironsides"

**September 8**
US cancels Dearborn-Prevost armistice

**October 13**
Battle of Queenston Heights; British Maj.-Gen. Sir Isaac Brock killed

**October 13**
Great Britain authorizes general reprisals against US

**October 18**
US Sloop *Wasp* defeats HM Sloop *Frolic*, but surrenders to HMS *Poictiers* in North Atlantic

**October 25**
USS *United States* captures HMS *Macedonian* in North Atlantic

**November 17**
US Brig. Gen. Alexander Smyth proclaims unauthorized plan to annex Canada

**November 19**
US invades Lower Canada (Quebec)

**November 23**
US withdraws from Lower Canada

**December 29**
USS *Constitution* defeats HMS *Java* off coast of Brazil

# 1813 WE HAVE MET THE ENEMY...

**US Maj. Gen. William Henry Harrison at the Battle of the Thames.**

**January 18 & 22**
First and Second Battles of Frenchtown/River Raisin

**January 23**
Great Britain's Native allies execute American prisoners in "River Raisin Massacre"

**February 6**
Great Britain proclaims blockade of Delaware and Chesapeake bays, targeting important trade and privateer ports

**February 24**
US Sloop *Hornet* sinks HMS *Peacock* off the coast of Guiana

**March 8**
Russia offers to mediate end to War of 1812

**March 10**
First runaway slaves in Chesapeake Bay seek refuge on HMS *Victorious*

**April 6**
Great Britain bombards Lewes, Delaware

**April 27**
Battle of York; US captures and burns Upper Canada's capital at York (Ontario)

**May 1–9**
First Siege of Fort Meigs, Ohio

**May 3**
Great Britain burns Havre de Grace, Maryland, destroying two-thirds of the town and sparking fears for the safety of the US capital

**May 26**
Great Britain extends blockade to major ports in middle and southern states

**May 27**
US captures Fort George, Upper Canada (Ontario)

**May 29**
Battle of Sackets Harbor, New York

**June 1**
HMS *Shannon* defeats USS *Chesapeake* off coast of Massachusetts

**June 5–6**
Battle of Stoney Creek, New York

**June 22**
Battle of Craney Island, Virginia

# 1813

**June 22–23**
Laura Secord's trek to warn British forces of planned American attack on Beaver Dams outpost

**June 24**
Battle of Beaver Dams, Upper Canada (Ontario)

**June 25**
Great Britain attacks Hampton, Virginia

**July 8**
British-allied Sauk stage final seige of Fort Madison, Missouri Territory (Iowa), in the war's only battle west of the Mississippi River

**Taskanugi Hatke (William McIntosh), a leader of the Lower Creeks, allied his warriors with American forces during the Creek War.**

**July 21–28**
Second siege of Fort Meigs, Ohio

**July 27**
Creek War begins with Battle of Burnt Corn, Mississippi Territory (Alabama)

**August 1–2**
Battle of Fort Stephenson, Ohio

**August 14**
HMS *Pelican* captures USS *Argus* in the Irish Sea

**August 30**
Battle of Fort Mims, Mississippi Territory (Alabama)

**September 10**
Battle of Lake Erie/Put-in-Bay, Ohio

**September 27**
US reoccupies Fort Detroit and occupies Fort Amherstburg (Malden), Upper Canada (Ontario)

**October 5**
Battle of the Thames/Moraviantown, Upper Canada (Ontario); Tecumseh killed

**October 26**
Battle of Châteauguay, Lower Canada (Quebec)

**November 3**
Battle of Tallushatchee, Mississippi Territory (Alabama)

**November 4**
Great Britain offers US direct peace negotiations

**November 9**
Battle of Talladega, Mississippi Territory (Alabama)

**November 11**
Battle of Crysler's Farm, Upper Canada (Ontario)

**November 16**
Great Britain extends blockade to Long Island Sound and remaining ports in middle and southern states

**November 18**
East Tennessee militia attack Hillabee Creek towns along the Tallapoosa, Mississippi Territory (Alabama)

**November 29**
Battle of Autosee/Tallassee, Mississippi Territory (Alabama)

**December 17**
US adopts embargo barring all US ships and goods from leaving port

**December 19**
Great Britain captures Fort Niagara, New York

**December 19–21**
Great Britain burns Lewiston, Youngstown, and Manchester, New York

**December 23**
Battle of Econochaca/Holy Ground, Mississippi Territory (Alabama)

**December 30**
Great Britain burns Buffalo and Black Rock, New York

# 1814 A FIGHT FOR OUR NATIONAL EXISTENCE...

**American forces occupying Fort Erie in Upper Canada repulse one of several British attempts to retake the fort during one of the bloodiest campaigns in the war.**

**January 22**
Battle of Emuckfau Creek, Mississippi Territory (Alabama)

**January 24**
Battle of Enitachopco Creek, Mississippi Territory (Alabama)

**January 27**
Battle of Calabee Creek, Mississippi Territory (Alabama)

**March 27**
Battle of Horseshoe Bend/ Tohopeka, Mississippi Territory (Alabama)

**March 30**
Second Battle of Lacolle Mill, Lower Canada (Quebec)

**April 2**
Great Britain issues proclamation urging slaves in Chesapeake to join British forces in exchange for freedom

**April 25**
Great Britain extends blockade to New England

**May 30**
Battle of Sandy Creek, New York

**May 30**
Napoleonic Wars suspended, allowing Great Britain to redeploy veteran forces to North America

**July 3**
US captures Fort Erie, Upper Canada (Ontario)

**July 5**
Battle of Chippewa, Upper Canada (Ontario)

**July 17–20**
Siege of Prairie du Chien, Illinois Territory (Wisconsin)

**July 22**
US and Miamis, Potawatomis, Ottawas, Shawnees, Kickapoos sign peace treaty at Greenville, Ohio

**July 25**
Battle of Lundy's Lane, Upper Canada (Ontario)

# 1814

**August 4**
US attacks Fort Mackinac, Michigan Territory

**August 8**
Peace negotiations between US and Great Britain begin at Ghent, Belgium

**August 9**
US and Creek sign peace treaty at Fort Jackson, Mississippi Territory (Alabama)

**August 9–11**
Battle of Stonington, Connecticut

**August 14**
Great Britain occupies Pensacola and Fort San Carlos de Barrancas, West Florida

**August 15**
Battle of Fort Erie, Upper Canada (Ontario)

**August 19–20**
Great Britain lands at Benedict, Maryland, en route to Washington, DC

**August 24**
Battle of Bladensburg, Maryland

**August 24–25**
Great Britain burns Washington, DC

**August 31**
Great Britain launches second major offensive with invasion of New York

**September 1–11**
Great Britain occupies 100 miles of US coast from Eastport to Castine, Maine

**September 11**
Battle of Lake Champlain, New York

**September 12**
Battle of North Point, Maryland

**September 13–14**
Great Britain bombards Fort McHenry

**September 14**
Francis Scott Key writes "The Star-Spangled Banner"

**September 15**
Battle of Fort Bowyer/Mobile Bay, West Florida (Alabama)

**October 21**
Britain offers peace on basis of *uti possidetis* (retaining territories held at the time of the treaty) after failure of Chesapeake and New York invasions

**October 22–November 17**
US Brig. Gen. Duncan McArthur's Raid into Upper Canada

**November 5**
US evacuates Fort Erie, Upper Canada (Ontario)

**November 7**
US occupies Pensacola, West Florida

**November 27**
Great Britain drops *uti possidetis* demand in peace negotiations

**December 14**
Battle of Lake Borgne, Louisiana

**December 15–January 5**
New England "secessionists" meet at Hartford Convention to articulate opposition

**December 23**
Battle of Villeré's Plantation/ Night Engagement at New Orleans

**December 24**
US and Great Britain finalize peace terms in Treaty of Ghent

**Militiamen in Philadelphia's First and Second Company of Union Guards wore shakos, or leather infantry caps, like this one when they were mustered into service in September 1814.**

# 1815 THE REPUBLIC IS SAFE...

**January 1**
Battle of Rodriguez Canal/
Artillery duel at New Orleans

**January 8**
Battle of New Orleans/
Chalmette; British Lieut. Gen.
Sir Edward Pakenham killed

**January 9-18**
Battle of Fort St. Philip,
Louisiana

**January 13**
Great Britain attacks
Point Peter/St. Marys on
Cumberland Island, Georgia

**January 16**
HMS *Endymion, Tenados,*
and *Pomone* capture USS
*President* outside of New
York Harbor

**February 8–11**
Siege of Fort Bowyer, West
Florida (Alabama)

**February 16**
War of 1812 ends when US
Senate approves Treaty of
Ghent and President Madison
ratifies the treaty as law

**February 20**
USS *Constitution* captures
HMS *Cyane* and HMS *Levant*
off Africa's Atlantic coast

**February 24**
Battle of St. Marys River,
Georgia

**March 13**
Official news of peace
reaches New Orleans; US
Maj. Gen. Andrew Jackson
lifts martial law

**March 20**
Napoleonic Wars resume with
Napoleon's assumption of
power

**March 23**
US Sloop *Hornet* captures
HM Sloop *Penguin* in South
Atlantic

**March 28**
News of peace reaches
London

**April 6**
Dartmoor Massacre, England

**June 18**
Battle of Waterloo, Belgium

**June 22**
Napoleonic Wars end with
Napoleon's abdication

**June 30**
Last battle of War of 1812:
US Sloop *Peacock* defeats
East India cruiser *Nautilus* in
Indian Ocean

**July 18–October 28**
US, Potawatomis,
Piankashaws, Teton Sioux,
Sioux of the Lakes, Yankton
Sioux, Omahas, Kickapoos,
Osages, Sauks, Foxes, Iowas,
and Kansas sign peace
treaties at Portage des Sioux,
Missouri Territory

**September 8**
US and Chippewas, Ottawas,
Potawatomis sign peace
treaty at Spring Wells,
Michigan Territory

# LEGACY

The treaties that ended the
war between the United
States and its British and
Native adversaries brought
a sense of victory to Americans. The United States
successfully negotiated an
end to the conflict with the
"conqueror of Europe,"
and acquired millions of
acres of Indian territory. But
America's "second war of
independence" left many
within the new nation with
an unfulfilled promise of
freedom. Before memories
of the War of 1812 could
fade into the distant past,
westward expansion and Indian Removal, together with
the institution of slavery and
a bloody civil war, would
continue to test America's
democratic experiment.

Boundary uncertain

LAKE SUPERIOR

Fort Mack

La Baye

LAKE MICHIGAN

MI
TE

Fort Shelby/McKay

Prairie du Chien

MISSOURI
TERRITORY

Battle of

Fort Dearborn

Fort D
Fort Way

Fort Madison

Fort Johnson

Prophet's Town

OLD NO

IND

Fort Osage

Mississippi

ILLINOIS
TERRITORY

Fort Ha
TERRI

Missouri

Fort
Bellefontaine

Vincennes

Saint Louis

Ohio

UNITED STATE

TENNE

Tennessee

Fort Strothe

Coos

Fort Williams

MISSISSIPPI
TERRITORY

Fort Jackso

LOUISIANA

Alabama

Fort
Stoddert

Fort Min

WEST FL

Area disputed by
United States and Spain

New Orleans

Pensa

Fort
Bowyer

Battle of New Orleans
Chalmette

Fort
Saint Philip

MEXICO

GULF OF MEX

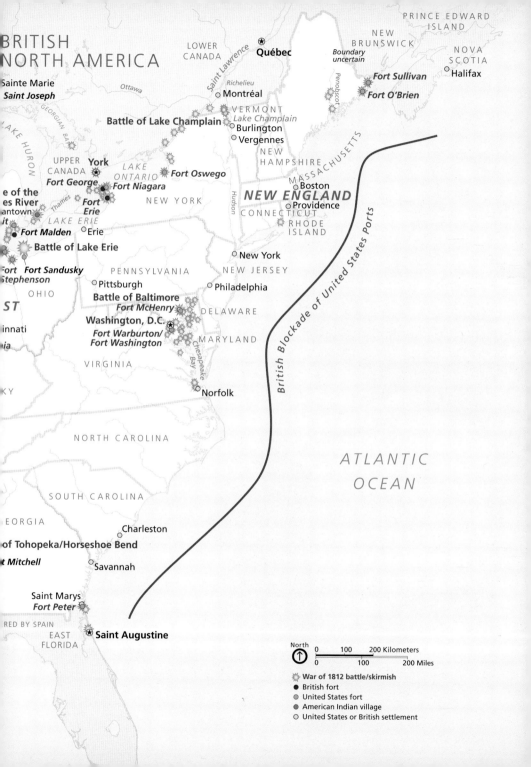

# From the American Revolution to the War of 1812

By Alan Taylor

*The War of 1812 served as the final act of the American Revolution, which was a complex and prolonged drama that lingered for a generation beyond the peace treaty of 1783 and the Federal Constitution of 1787. During the revolution, the American patriots risked their new nation on a republic, then a risky and radical form of government where sovereignty derived from a broad electorate. In a second great gamble, they sought to sustain that new republic on a vast and unprecedented scale: the eastern third of a continent.*

Many Americans, and more Europeans, doubted that any republic could endure but especially not one so large and diverse. Inevitably, the critics expected the various states violently to separate and perhaps then pass under the imperial domination of Spain, France, or Britain.

Despising the new republic, the British and their American loyalist supporters celebrated the mixed constitution of Great Britain—the combination of commons, lords, and monarch—as more stable, just, and powerful. Where the American patriots sought to disperse and reduce the power of government, the British sustained an empire with the coercive "energy" to wage war and to regulate the liberty of common people.

By British standard, the United States was a flimsy union of discordant states: a virtual nullity. A British spy, John Henry, dismissed the republic as "that crazy coalition of heterogeneous interests, opinions and prejudices." Referring to the number of states and their weak union, Henry concluded, "Seventeen staves and no hoop will not make a

> *"Seventeen staves and no hoop will not make a barrell that can last long."*

**The Treaty of Paris, negotiated by a delegation led by Ben Franklin, may have ended America's War of Independence from Great Britain, but the political revolution in the new republic had only begun.**

barrell that can last long." According to British officials, the foolish Americans lived in a fantasy republic that pandered to their illusion that they need neither pay for, nor obey, their federal government.

The British also regarded Americans as doubly damned for owning black men while preaching the equality of white men. To Britons, it seemed odd that race mattered so much, and class so little, in the distribution of political rights in America. In sum, British officials disliked the republic as weak, chaotic, corrupt, rancorous, vulgar, and demagogic. A Canadian prelate, John Strachan, concluded, "Liberty in such a country becomes worse than an empty name, a mask for oppression."

After the revolution, the British Empire and the United States remained uneasy neighbors in North America. During the 1780s and 1790s, the British built a counterrevolutionary regime in Canada, beginning with 40,000 American loyalists expelled by the patriot victory. In Upper Canada (now Ontario), they sought to set an example of superior stability and prosperity that eventually would entice the rebel Americans to forsake their dangerous experiment in republican government. Loyalists did not believe that the British Empire had permanently lost the fight against the American Revolution.

Neither Britons nor Americans thought that their rival political systems could coexist for long in a shared continent. Britons predicted that the republic inevitably would collapse into anarchy and civil war. Surely repentant Americans would then beg for readmission into the empire. With equal conviction, Americans insisted that nature destined their republic to dominate the continent. Eventually, they predicted, the Canadians would join the United States by rejecting the artificial rule of a foreign empire. Created by the revolution, the border between the republic and the empire seemed tenuous and temporary: destined to shift either north or south as one or the other collapsed. Ironically, until 1812, the parallel convictions of inevitable collapse kept relations tense but short of war, for why risk blood and treasure on an invasion when the rival's collapse would come naturally in due time?

*The political partisans were so shrill because the stakes seemed so high: the survival of the republic and its tenuous union of fractious states.*

The slow drift to the new war in North America began with the French Revolution of 1789. Four years later, the British joined the coalition of European monarchies waging war to destroy the radical French republic created by that revolution. During the 1790s, Americans became

entangled in the new global war between the French and British, whose fleets and armies fought in every ocean and on almost every continent. Each great power pressured the weaker United States for assistance against the other belligerent. The British played upon the American economic dependence on British imports and on the vulnerability of American merchant ships to the might of the Royal Navy. The French appealed to the Americans as fellow republicans in a shared global struggle against monarchs and aristocrats.

The global and ideological conflict widened a political rift within the United States between the two major parties: the Federalists and the Republicans. During the 1790s, the Federalists held national power, controlling the Congress and the presidency under George Washington and John Adams. But they faced growing opposition from the Republicans led by Thomas Jefferson and James Madison (these Republicans cannot be equated with the contemporary Republican party, which first emerged during the 1850s). The political partisans were so shrill because the stakes seemed so high: the survival of the republic and its tenuous union of fractious states. Although endowed with an immense potential for economic and demographic growth, the United States was then a new and weak republic in a dangerous world of powerful empires.

**Governing can be contentious. As political factions formed during the 1790s, Federalist Roger Griswold and Democratic-Republican Matthew Lyon fought with cane and fire tongs on the floor of the House of Representatives.**

Neither the Federalists nor the Republicans accepted the legitimacy of the other party. Both cast their opponents as a selfish and destructive faction bent on perverting the fragile republic. Ironically, that dread of parties drove each group to practice an especially bitter partisanship. Claiming exclusively to speak for the people, each party cast rivals as insidious conspirators bent on destroying freedom and the union.

As the more conservative party, the Federalists sought greater social stability and national power—at the expense of the states. During the 1790s, the Federalists established a national bank, consolidated a national debt, built an army and navy, and funded their expensive initiatives with increased taxes. The Federalists agreed with Britons that a true nation needed a central authority invested with the power to act with energy.

The Republicans favored a minimal federal government and a decentralized union, where most power remained with the states. They insisted that dispersing power would prevent the emergence of an American aristocracy to dominate a national government. Equality and consent, not central command, should unite the people. Of course, Federalists rejected the Republican vision as dangerously naive and doomed to collapse into anarchy.

The Republicans and Federalists also clashed over the proper degree of democracy needed to sustain the national republic. The Federalists insisted that common people should elect, and then defer to, a paternalistic elite defined by their superior education, wealth, and status. Once elected, gentlemen should govern free from "licentious" criticism that eroded public esteem for them. In sharp contrast, the Republicans promised to heed public opinion and to deny special privileges to any elite. They insisted that equal rights and opportunity would elevate the industrious poor rather than perpetuate the idle rich.

But, while pushing for equal rights for white men, most Republicans disdained Indians and African Americans. In their racial hierarchy, all white men were equal in their rights and superior to all blacks and natives. By comparison, the more elitist Federalists treated Indians and blacks as worthy of some paternalism and protection. To appeal for white votes, the Republicans derided the Federalists as pro-black and pro-Indian.

**Teyoninhokovrawen, Major John Norton, lived in multiple worlds. Born in Scotland, he joined the British Army, moved to Canada, was adopted by the Mohawk community, and defended Canada against American invasion.**

It was true during the War of 1812, and remains so today. There is no guarantee that personal and ethnic loyalties match international borders. Irish immigrants to North America, for example, served in both the US and British armies. French Canadians filled the ranks of volunteer Voltigeur units in Lower Canada at the same time that Great Britain fought Napoleon in Europe. Many former American colonists as well as enslaved men and women seeking emancipation chose to resettle in the British Empire after the American Revolution. Three thousand "Black Loyalists," evacuated from New York City, moved to Nova Scotia. Families divided by war remained unreconciled in peace. Siblings and cousins lived on both sides of the border.

The homelands of native peoples bore little resemblance to European-imposed boundaries and native aspirations only coincidentally meshed with the political goals of Washington, DC, or London. John Norton (Teyoninhokovrawen) had a Cherokee father and a Scottish mother. Educated in Scotland but adopted by the Haudenosaunee (Iroquois) after he came to North America, Norton allied with the British and led Mohawk warriors against the Americans at the battles of Queenston Heights, Stoney Creek, and Chippawa.

Unresolved by the Treaty of Ghent that ended the War of 1812, borderland conflict between the United States and Canada flared into occasional violence from Maine to Oregon and along the Niagara Frontier. Only the passage of time, multiple treaties, and on-again, off-again negotiation slowly tamed tensions and redefined loyalties.

USS *Chesapeake* proudly flew a pennant that read "Free Trade and Sailors' Rights," shorthand for American grievances. Following a furious, 15-minute battle in 1813, *Chesapeake* surrendered to HMS *Shannon*.

The French Revolution reignited the debate among Americans over the proper meaning of their own still unsettled revolution. The Republicans identified with France as a sister republic assailed by the monarchies of Europe, but the Federalists denounced the French Revolution as dangerously radical and violent. Both the Federalists and the Republicans favored preserving American neutrality in the global conflict, but each group accused the other of covertly undermining that neutrality. The Republicans feared that a British triumph would embolden the Federalists to undermine the republican institutions in America. The Federalists similarly dreaded that a French victory would unleash a new and more radical revolution within the United States. Both parties exaggerated the danger posed by the other. In fact, the Republicans were not French-style radicals, and the Federalists were not aristocratic loyalists. But both parties acted on their lurid fears rather than on a dispassionate examination of the facts.

In the election of 1800–1801, the Republicans swept the Federalists from national power. Jefferson became president and worked to weaken the federal government and to empower the states. He cut taxes, reduced the military, and paid down the national debt. Jefferson also ousted free blacks from federal jobs and accelerated the dispossession of Indians. Sidelined, the Federalists seethed and longed for an opportunity to return to power—but in 1808 the Republicans elected Madison to succeed his friend Jefferson as president.

Meanwhile, relations with Great Britain worsened over the growing American commerce with France and her colonies. By 1807, the French Revolution had collapsed in a coup that elevated a military genius and despot, Napoleon Bonaparte, who created an empire from the ruins of the French republic. Rather than make peace with the British, Napoleon escalated the war, conquering most of Europe. To undermine the French economy, the British sought to enforce a strict blockade on foreign commerce, to the detriment of American merchant ships, for British naval captains profited by confiscating any neutral ships en route to or from trading with the French and their allies.

The British also desperately needed more sailors to man the vast Royal Navy required to blockade Europe and to control the shipping lanes of the world. To get those sailors, British naval officers stopped neutral merchant ships to "impress" into their service any men who seemed to be British by birth. Often those impressed sailors had left the British Isles to seek the higher pay and better conditions of American merchant ships. Sometimes, however, the naval officers seized Americans by birth. In that first generation after the revolution, it was often difficult to distinguish Americans from Britons—and naval captains did not care to try when they had pressing vacancies in their ships.

Although offended by the British seizures of ships and impressment of sailors, President Jefferson and his secretary of state, James Madison, balked at declaring war, for they feared the high costs and heavy taxes of building up the military. After all, they had risen to national power by exploiting the unpopularity of the Federalist taxes to fund a bigger army and navy.

Rather than build more warships, the Republicans waged a commercial war by suspending all American trade with the world in an "embargo" that began in December 1807.

European politics, particularly the French Revolution and then Napoleon's rise to power, further divided emerging party factions in the United States.

Heart of Oak
Well Tommy! I brought you
at last to close Quarters therefore
mind what you are about!— If you
dont behave gently Ill break your
limbs and leave you the rest.
let me tell you my Boy,
keep yourself Cool!

*The failure of the embargo left the Republicans with two stark alternatives: wage war or submit to British domination on the high seas.*

By locking down all American ships in their ports, the Republicans sought to pressure the British into relinquishing impressment and the strict blockade. Jefferson and Madison reasoned that the British economy would collapse without food imported from America and without access to the American market for British manufactures. In fact, the British found alternative markets in Latin America. Indeed, the embargo inflicted greater damage on the American economy. In turn, that pain revived the Federalist party in the northeast, the region that most relied on overseas commerce. The dismayed Republicans lifted the embargo in March 1809, just as Jefferson retired and Madison became president.

The failure of the embargo left the Republicans with two stark alternatives: wage war or submit to British domination on the high seas. The Federalists favored tacit submission as more profitable and less dangerous—given the shrunken and demoralized state of the American military cut to the bone by Jefferson. But in early 1812, Madison and bellicose congressmen, known as War Hawks, decided that submitting to British naval domination eroded American sovereignty and imperilled national honor. Averse to the high costs of a bigger navy, the Republicans also hoped to win a war on the cheap by invading and conquering Canada with a new army of volunteers drawn from the state militias.

Conquering Canada also promised to stifle the armed resistance by Indians to westward expansion by American settlers. In the frontier zone south of the Great Lakes, Indians had obtained encouragement and munitions from British traders and officers based in nearby Canada. Republicans insisted that the natives should be their dependents living within a fixed boundary separating British from American sovereignty. But the British treated the Indians as independent peoples dwelling in their own country between the empire and the republic—and thereby free to make their own alliances.

By saving the Indian nations from American destruction, the British hoped to preserve valuable allies for a future, and apparently inevitable, war with the Americans. But that low-level assistance became a self-fulfilling prophecy as the Republicans insisted that the British caused the Indian resistance. In newspapers and Congress, the Republicans blamed the atrocities of frontier war on the British—and vowed to drive them from their bases in Canada.

Despite the nation's military weakness, most Republicans felt that they had to declare war or lose their credibility. They also desperately hoped that war would galvanize and unify a divided country. Madison later explained that "he knew the unprepared state of the country, but he esteemed it necessary to throw forward the flag of the country, sure that the people would press forward and defend it." By uniting the country behind a war, and by casting the Federalists as pro-British traitors, the Republicans hoped to ruin their opponents once and for all.

The Federalists opposed the war as a military folly in service to a moral travesty, for they favored the British crusade to defeat Napoleon, aptly deemed a bloody dictator who threatened the rest of the world. Launched at the peak of Napoleon's power, the new American war might help the dictator to defeat the British. In addition, the Federalists dreaded the retaliatory power of the Royal Navy to sweep American ships from the seas and to bombard American seaports.

The Federalists vowed to undermine the war effort, hastening the inevitable American defeats that, they hoped, would discredit the Republicans as inept and corrupt. Disabused of their illusions, the voters would then return the Federalists to power and the nation to peace—so the Federalists dreamed. In the meantime, Federalist merchants meant to profit by smuggling with the British, providing provisions desperately needed by the British garrisons in Canada. In New England, some Federalists even flirted with secession and overtures to the British for a separate peace.

In 1812 Britain's rulers wanted to avoid a war in America as a dangerous distraction from the pressing struggle against Napoleon. But the British would never relinquish their power to stop and search neutral merchant ships to regulate trade and to seize runaway subjects. And, once forced into a war in North America, the British resolved to teach the Americans a bloody lesson that would undermine their confidence in republican government. The war promised to determine the survival of the American union and republic—and therefore the meaning and success (or failure) of the American Revolution.

*A professor of history at the University of California at Davis, Alan Taylor is the author of* The Civil War of 1812: American Citizens, British Subjects, Irish Rebels, & Indian Allies *(New York: Alfred A. Knopf, 2010).*

**Top:** Because Kentucky depended on trade that passed through the port of New Orleans, Congressman Richard Johnson joined the chorus that clamored for war with Great Britain.

**Bottom:** In hindsight, Virginian John Randolph appears clairvoyant. A fiery opponent of the War of 1812, he predicted the "ruin of our country." "Before you conquer Canada," he said, "the Capitol will be a ruin."

# The Global Context of the War of 1812

By Donald R. Hickey

*Americans remember the War of 1812 as a second war of independence, as a war to force the British to give up practices that violated American rights and undermined US sovereignty. But this war was a byproduct of a much larger conflict in Europe.*

In what is sometimes called the Second Hundred Years War (1689–1815), Great Britain and France fought off and on for more than a century to determine which nation would dominate Europe and the wider world. In the final round of this contest—the Napoleonic Wars (1803–1815)—Great Britain adopted maritime practices that caused the War of 1812. Far from being isolated from events in Europe, the War of 1812 was a direct outgrowth of the Napoleonic Wars.

After Vice Admiral Horatio Nelson's great victory over the French and Spanish fleets off the coast of Portugal in the Battle of Trafalgar (1805), Great Britain was undisputed "Mistress of the Seas." But because Napoleon won an equally decisive battle six weeks later at Austerlitz (in the modern Czech Republic), France was now master of the Continent. With each belligerent supreme in its element, the only way they could wage war was by targeting one another's trade. As the leading neutral with a large and far-flung overseas commerce, the United States got caught in the middle of this trade war.

On Christmas Eve 1814, in the city of Ghent, John Quincy Adams shook hands with British Admiral of the Fleet James Gambler, concluding peace negotiations with a treaty that failed to mention the maritime policies that caused the war or to recognize any territorial gains.

Because Great Britain controlled the seas, her encroachments on American rights were considered more serious. The two leading causes of the War of 1812 were the Orders-in-Council, British decrees which sharply curtailed American trade with the European Continent, and impressment, which was the British practice of conscripting seamen from American merchant vessels. Although

Optimistically, the United States thought it would teach both Great Britain and France a thing or two about respect. In this 1813 print, Columbia (US) reminds John Bull (Great Britain) and Napoleon (France) of early American naval victories, but both adversaries proved to be difficult pupils.

the Royal Navy sought to confine impressment to British subjects, many Americans—probably around 6,000 between 1803 and 1812—were caught in the dragnet. These maritime policies had a direct and significant impact on the United States, but their primary purpose was to further Britain's war effort against Napoleonic France.

When the United States declared war on June 18, 1812, there was some hope among Republican leaders that the news would bring the British to their senses and that they would cave in to American demands. The nation's war aims might thus be won without any fighting. If combat operations were necessary, the fledgling republic could hardly hope to defeat the British on the high seas. The only alternative was to strike at Britain's North American provinces in Canada and hope to use territory conquered here as a bargaining chip to secure concessions on the maritime issues. Some Americans, especially in the West, were eager to target Canada for another reason: they hoped to permanently drive Britain from North America and thus eliminate a powerful rival and put an end to British influence over American Indians.

The conquest of most of Canada was expected to be, in the words of Thomas Jefferson, "a mere matter of marching." The United States had a huge population advantage—7.7 million to 500,000—and many people living north of the border—the original French population and recent American immigrants who had moved to Canada to take advantage of free land and low taxes—were not expected to put up much of a fight. Many Republicans anticipated what antiwar critic John Randolph of Virginia called "a holiday campaign." With "no expense of blood, or treasure, on our part—Canada is to conquer herself—she is to be subdued by the principles of fraternity."

Few Americans anticipated how difficult a Canadian campaign might be. Although the bulk of the British army was tied up in the Spanish Peninsula, the small force charged with protecting Canada was ably led and combat tested and was aided in no small manner by Britain's Indian allies. These included various tribes in the Old Northwest led by two Shawnee brothers, Tecumseh and the Prophet, and the Grand River Iroquois (Haudenosaunee) in Upper Canada (now Ontario) under the leadership of a Scottish-Cherokee mixed-blood, John Norton, whose native name was Teyoninhokovrawen but who was popularly known as "the Snipe." Americans also underestimated the stupendous logistical problems of waging war in a distant wilderness, the profound lack of readiness of an American army filled with amateur officers and untried enlisted men, and the lack of dependability of a militia that had little discipline or training and even less taste for battle, especially outside the United States.

The young republic was unable to overcome these obstacles, and the invasions of 1812 and 1813 ended in failure. The only bright spots were in the West. In the Old Northwest Master Commandant Oliver H. Perry's victory on Lake Erie in 1813 paved the way for Major General William Henry Harrison's victory in the Battle of the Thames. Harrison's victory established American dominance in the region, shattered the Indian confederacy, and led to Tecumseh's death. Major General Andrew Jackson secured a similar dominion over the Old Southwest with a series of victories over the Creeks. The western victories were undoubtedly significant because they paved the way for American expansion, but they were too far from the centers of power further east to alter the course of the war with Great Britain.

There were several spectacular American naval victories on the high seas, most notably by the US Frigate *Constitution*, but these were in single-ship duels of little strategic consequence. American warships and privateers also took a heavy toll on British commerce. Great Britain found these losses annoying but hardly a reason to make peace. The

*Few Americans anticipated how difficult a Canadian campaign might be.*

In September 1814, with France out of the war in Europe and the United States now fighting a war for "national existence," Thomas Macdonough turned back a British invasion of New York at the Battle of Lake Champlain.

British responded to the affronts at sea by imposing an ever more extensive blockade on the American coast, which undermined American prosperity and cut sharply into government revenue. Although Americans might be justly proud of their showing in the West and at sea, after two years of campaigning, the war was essentially a stalemate. Canada remained in British hands, and the United States was no closer to victory.

By the time the campaigning season in 1814 opened, the tide had turned against Napoleon in Europe, and this had a profound impact on the war in America. Napoleon's invasion of Russia in June 1812 had ended in disaster, and in October 1813 Britain's allies on the Continent won a major victory at Leipzig (in what is now Germany). With the war on the Continent turning against Napoleon, the British in late 1813 began cautiously redeploying forces to America, and thereafter their prospects in both wars—in Europe and in America—steadily improved.

While Britain's allies on the Continent (who were part of the Sixth Coalition) pursued Napoleon to Paris from the east, the Duke of Wellington fought his way into France from the Spanish Peninsula in the south. By the spring of 1814, France had had enough. Napoleon abdicated unconditionally and was exiled to the Mediterranean island of Elba. With the restoration of peace in Europe, the British could step up the redeployment of their military and naval assets to the American war and take the offensive. This fundamentally changed the character of the War of 1812. "We should have to fight hereafter," said one Republican, "not for 'free trade and sailors' rights,' not for the conquest of the Canadas, but for our national existence."

> *"We should have to fight hereafter, not for 'free trade and sailors rights,' not for the conquest of the Canadas, but for our national existence."*

In the campaign of 1814, the United States remained on the offensive on the Niagara frontier, and the result was a series of bloody but inconclusive battles—at Chippawa, Lundy's Lane, and Fort Erie. Further east, the young republic was thrown on the defensive. The British enjoyed some success, seizing a hundred miles of the coast of Maine and the Nation's Capital in Washington and burning the public buildings there, but elsewhere they were rebuffed. An inland naval victory engineered by Master Commandant Thomas Macdonough on Lake Champlain forced the British to give up a major invasion of New York. At the same time, the construction of extensive earthworks combined with the successful defense of Fort McHenry compelled them to abandon a planned assault on Baltimore.

In early 1815, the British invaded the Gulf Coast, where the United States appeared to be particularly vulnerable. New Orleans, which was the biggest port city in the West, was largely undefended, and the population, which was heavily French and Spanish, felt no loyalty to the young republic. "The War of the U.S. is very unpopular with us," John Windship, a transplanted New Englander, reported in early 1814. French and Spanish residents who were called up for militia duty in New Orleans "absolutely refused to be marched" and "declared themselves liege [feudal] subjects of Spain or France." Spain, which was allied to Great Britain, had never been happy with the Louisiana Purchase, and there was talk that the British might seize the entire territory and return it to Spain. Although the British were only interested in seizing territory that might be used in the peace negotiations, Andrew Jackson prevented even this

The Battle of New Orleans, seen here from the British perspective, presented a shocking defeat to nearly 8,000 seasoned veterans and dealt the most crushing defeat of the entire war. Within hours of the massive frontal assault on American defenses, British plans to occupy New Orleans lay dying with their commander Lieut. Gen. Sir Edward Pakenham, at center.

with his victory at New Orleans. "Old Hickory's" triumph was not simply the most lopsided of the war but one of the most lopsided defeats ever suffered by a British army in any war. The British lost over 2,000 killed, wounded, missing, or captured, while Jackson's losses were only 70.

Just as the course of the war was influenced by developments in Europe, so, too, were the peace negotiations. The two warring nations sent peace delegations to Ghent in modern-day Belgium for talks that got under way in August 1814. Because the British had scrapped the Orders-in-Council shortly after war had been declared, the only major outstanding issue was impressment. By the time the talks began, the United States had dropped this issue, which seemed

to pave the way for peace. But the British were now in the driver's seat and laid out their own terms for peace.

The British demanded the establishment of an Indian barrier state in the Old Northwest, territorial concessions in northern Maine and present-day Minnesota, the American demilitarization of the Great Lakes, and an end to American fishing privileges in Canadian waters. These demands, which were designed mainly to protect Canada and Britain's Indian allies from renewed aggression from the south, were what one scholar has called "a probing operation." Their purpose was to provide a basis for negotiation and to determine what concessions the United States might be willing to make.

When the Americans held firm against these demands, the British offered peace on the basis of *uti possidetis*, which meant that each side would keep any territory it held when the treaty was signed. If this offer were accepted, the British probably would have bartered away coastal Maine to secure control of a few strategically located forts further west. When the US delegation balked at this offer, the British retreated again and ultimately agreed in the Treaty of Ghent to restore the *status quo ante bellum*—the state that existed before the war.

The British dropped their demands in part because of the lack of military progress in America. Although buoyed by the occupation of Washington, they soon learned that their forces had withdrawn from New York and given up the assault on Baltimore. There was also growing discontent at home over the tax burden. Another year of campaigning was likely to cost £10 million ($49 million), and this would necessitate continuing the onerous war taxes that were still in place from the French war. No less important was an ominous impasse in the negotiations at the Congress of Vienna, which had convened in September 1814 to forge a peace settlement in Europe. Indeed, at one point British leaders were considering how quickly they could recall troops from the New World to buttress their position in the Old.

When the British ministry asked the Duke of Wellington to take command in America, the "Iron Duke" agreed to do so, but not until the following spring. More importantly, he told the government that it had no right to demand territorial concessions in America without control of the Great Lakes. This opinion gave British leaders all the cover they needed to end the war without any territorial gains. Lord Castlereagh, Britain's foreign secretary, congratulated

Prime Minister Lord Liverpool on "being released from the millstone of an American war," and a British official at Vienna reported that the news of peace had "produced an astonishing effect," helping to foil a Russian bid for aggrandizement. All agreed that without the distraction of a war in North America, Britain's hand in Europe was strengthened. Events in Europe, which had caused the War of 1812 and then shaped its course, now helped bring it to an end.

The news of peace was greeted in America with relief, and there were celebrations and parades across the republic. Even the most ardent War Hawk showed no interest in continuing a war that had turned decidedly sour and now offered little prospect of any concrete gains. Under these circumstances everyone realized that a return to the *status quo ante bellum* was the best that the United States could hope for.

Most Americans do not remember that the war had ended in a draw on the battlefield or that the maritime issues that had caused it were not even mentioned in the peace treaty. Jackson's spectacular success at New Orleans, coupled with the naval victories on the high seas and the northern lakes, shaped the postwar memory of the conflict. Americans boasted of how they had "unqueened the self-stiled Queen of the Ocean," and defeated "Wellington's invincibles" and "the conquerors of the conquerors of Europe." They forgot the causes of the war and ignored how close they had come to defeat.

Americans also lost sight of how closely this war was tied to a much larger conflict in Europe. To the British, the contest was but one theater, and a decidedly minor one at that, in a multifaceted war that they were waging against the Crown's enemies on both sides of the Atlantic. Throughout this period, Britain's perspective was preeminently European. Her focus remained firmly riveted on the Continent, her top priority always being to prevent France or any nation from dominating Europe. That preoccupation not only caused the War of 1812; it also shaped the course of the war and influenced the terms upon which the British were willing to end it.

*Don Hickey, a professor of history at Wayne State College in Nebraska, is the author of six books on the War of 1812, most recently,* The Rockets' Red Glare: An Illustrated History of the War of 1812, *with Connie D. Clark (2011), and* The War of 1812: A Forgotten Conflict, Bicentennial Edition *(2012).*

**John Rubens Smith's *Peace* uses grandiose symbolism to celebrate the Treaty of Ghent. Columbia, at left, grasps the hand of her equal, Britannia, and these two representations of former adversaries extend olive branches as peace descends upon sailors who bear their national standards.**

# American Indians and the War of 1812

By Kathryn E. Holland Braund

*The Indian war which broke out in the Ohio country in 1811 and the Red Stick or Creek War of 1813 are commonly viewed as part of the War of 1812 and evidence of British treachery by enlisting "savage" Indian allies against Americans. In reality, the Indian wars were concurrent conflicts that had their origins in long-standing grievances over land and the right of Indian peoples to self-determination.*

American War Hawks (pro-war congressmen) pointed to the actions of the British Royal Navy in harming the American economy and impressing American sailors into the British service as the primary reason for going to war in 1812. But the sectional vote for war confirmed the on-the-ground reality that the war, at its crux, was about expansion and removing what westerners perceived as the Indian "menace," which in its most benign manifestation blocked expansion into desirable territory and at its worst resulted in bloody warfare against American settlements. Displacing or humbling the British in Canada and Spanish Florida were also objectives of many westerners who believed these powers presented a very real threat by way of Indian alliances. Indeed, Americans all along the frontier accused Britain of instigating Indian warfare against Americans.

The Shawnee and Creek wars of the period had roots in nearly two centuries of transition, conflict, and accommodation. Britain's first imperial Indian agent for the southern tribes, Edmund Atkin, famously dubbed the Shawnees the "greatest travellers in America" with good reason. Due to pressure from the powerful Iroquois, the Shawnees had moved from their original homelands in the Ohio Valley. By the late seventeenth century, groups of Shawnees were along the Savannah River in Georgia, which took its name

**Tenskwatawa, The Prophet, inspired a pan-Indian movement to return to traditional ways. He believed that the Americans were "children of the Evil Spirit" and, with his brother Tecumseh, allied a force of warriors with the British during the war.**

from them, and in Pennsylvania. By the mid-18th century, Shawnees had reoccupied the Ohio Valley while others settled among the Creek towns. More than a century of travels created ethnic diversity in the Shawnees' seasonal settlements and left the disparate Shawnee bands politically fragmented. In contrast, the relatively stable town sites of the Creeks ranged along major river valleys in what is now Alabama and Georgia. Primarily composed of Muskogean tribes, the Creeks welcomed refugees and remnant tribal groups, and their multiethnic confederacy was among the most powerful and wealthiest Indian nations east of the Mississippi. By the 19th century, annual meetings of headmen had evolved into a National Council that represented the ostensibly united towns.

These two Indian nations, although differing in many ways, had long connections. Not only had displaced Shawnees found refuge and established towns under the protection of the Creek confederacy, but Creek-Shawnee emissaries also visited each other periodically to discuss intertribal cooperation against white expansion.

Both tribes also engaged in commercial and cultural exchange, primarily through trading relationships with both the British and the French in the colonial era. Trade in deerskins, beaver pelts, and other forest products was part of a frontier exchange economy that brought a wealth of manufactured goods to Indian towns. A wide variety of cloth, from sturdy woolens to gaudy calicos, made up the bulk of the trade, but guns and tools were essential as well. Guns facilitated hunting, were viewed as essential for defense, and, as the latest imported technology, brought status to their Indian owners. Beads, silver jewelry, and other exotic items such as imported ostrich feathers provided a means for fashionable and artistic self-presentment that displayed individual wealth and status.

Although Indians viewed the products of the hunt as the property of the individual hunter, their ability to participate in the world market economy through trade depended on access to tribal hunting lands, which were owned in common. Indian tribes, even those who lived in established towns, claimed and defended vast territories over which they wielded an active, if not actual, possession of the land. By hunting, harvesting forest products, and utilizing natural resources, Indians had sustained themselves and via trade, brought both increased personal prosperity as well as collective debt to their towns and a dependence on outsiders.

The American Revolution largely remade the commercial world of Indian peoples. The ouster of the loyalist merchants and traders cut off Indians from their suppliers. Americans lacked access to the credit and trade connections that sustained the trading economy. A declining demand for Indian produce such as deerskins and a reduction in the numbers of game animals from overhunting irreparably damaged the old trading economy. And few European Americans wished to deal with Indians. Many tribes had sided with the British during the conflict, believing the British government more sympathetic to their land claims than colonists. Newly independent Americans, once free from British restraints against expansion into Indian territory after the war, and still angry about Indian-British alliances during the revolutionary conflict, were more concerned with farming than trading with culturally different people who, increasingly, were viewed as "savage" and "enemies."

This early 19th century depiction of indigenous peoples of Upper Canada illustrates the complex cultural and commercial exchange, including guns and ornamental items such as cloth and silver jewelry, that were part of trading relationships with European Americans during the colonial era.

Nearly two decades after Pennsylvania militia massacred Christian Lenape Indians at the Moravian mission at Gnadenhutten (Ohio) in 1782, Tecumseh reminded Americans of the murder of Indian men, women, and children "even as they prayed to Jesus."

After the American Revolution, the Washington administration embraced a program to "civilize" native peoples, transforming Indians from tribal peoples into individuals who could be easily assimilated into American society. The civilization program promoted commercial agriculture, Christianity, an alteration in the gender-based divisions of labor among Indians, and, most importantly, private ownership of land. Americans hoped that if Indian peoples settled down to farm life, they would have little need of vast hunting territories and would willingly cede this "excess" territory to Americans. The government also encouraged Indians to run up debts to traders and government stores. Indian debts, which outstripped their ability to pay, could then be settled by sale of tribal lands. Meanwhile, American agents used annuity payments as well as donations from Quakers and other religious groups to purchase plows and spinning wheels in their effort to transform the work roles of native men and women. Women, in particular, were key to the plan, which sought to introduce Indians to cloth production to end the dependence of cloth obtained through trade.

Indians themselves responded to changing economic conditions in creative ways. As overhunting decimated deer herds, domesticated animals, including cattle and pigs, appeared more frequently in the Creek landscape. Communal fields along the rich river banks gave way to smaller individual plots as Creek ranchers moved to the uplands seeking pasture for their animals. Cattle, horses, and slaves became as valuable market commodities as deerskins had once been. In southern Creek territory, along the border with the Mississippi Territory, families of mixed-Creek and European ancestry established farms, ferries, and increasingly created private wealth from communal lands. For the Shawnees, the primary focus of the civilization movement was at Wapokoneta, on the upper Auglaize River, where, under the leadership of Black Hoof, Shawnees were tutored by government agents and Quakers. As among the Creeks, the outsiders promoted commercial agriculture, instructed women in the domestic arts of spinning and weaving, and introduced livestock to Shawnee men. With changing economies came fundamental changes in the way men and women viewed themselves. Men, whose fame and self-worth had previously rested on skills as warriors and hunters now found new outlets for masculine expression via the market and as cattle ranchers. Some Indian women, whose responsibilities had always included the production of finished leather for household use as well as trade, willingly took up the loom.

*The Washington administration embraced a program to "civilize" native peoples, transforming Indians from tribal peoples into individuals who could be easily assimilated into American society.*

Even though some Indians began to hold new views of work and property, Indian peoples did not abandon their view that all the land was held jointly by their tribes and even those moving toward commercial agriculture and other pursuits were not inclined to part with the land. American views of private land ownership were at odds with the idea of community ownership. But it wasn't so much the nature of Indian landholding that did not sit well with white Americans as the fact that the land was owned by Indians, who were viewed as "savage" and racially inferior to white Americans. Escalating demands from more and more cessions of Indian land earned white people a new name among the Creeks: "ecunnaunuxulgee," "people greedily grasping after the lands of the red people."

In the years prior to the American Revolution, the British had attempted to end hostilities and confrontations with Indian tribes along the frontier by implementing a variety of measures to thwart settler encroachment on Indian lands. The Proclamation of 1763, the most notable of these measures, forbade settlement west of a line that sliced through the backcountry of Britain's Atlantic colonies. The British had sought to mark newly established boundaries between Indians and colonists to end boundary disputes. The boundaries negotiated by various tribes were meant to stand, at least in Indian eyes, as one Creek chief noted like "a stone wall never to be broke." By the early 19th century, tribes increasingly came to define themselves as territorial entities with permanent boundaries and the sovereign right to live independently and protect their borders. Although pushed relentlessly by American agents to cede more and more territory, they viewed their territorial boundaries as inviolate: Indian country was for Indian peoples.

American expansion was no myth. Georgia's population grew to a quarter million, nearly doubling in the first decade of the 19th century. To the west of Creek country, the Mississippi Territory was established in 1803. Not only did the white and black population grow rapidly there, but the numbers of people crossing Creek lands to reach Mississippi shot up as well. The Creek agent noted 3,700 people had moved along the Federal Road through Creek territory from the fall of 1811 through the early spring of 1812. The new states of Kentucky (1792), Tennessee (1796), and Louisiana (1812) clearly pointed the direction that Americans intended to pursue: settlement and establishment of American hegemony over territories that had once been Indian lands.

It was the same in the Ohio valley. The 1795 Treaty of Greenville, which ended, for a time, the conflicts between Shawnees and Americans, opened former Indian lands to settlement. The new American territory achieved statehood in 1803, and by 1810 Ohio's population of 230,000 was nearly that of Georgia. Further white expansion into the region had been made possible by the Treaty of Fort Wayne (1809) whereby accommodationist Delaware, Miami, and Potawatomi chiefs ceded over three million acres of hunting lands claimed by various Indian tribes to the United States in return for annuities. Other tribes who held claims on the area ultimately ratified the proceedings, but only under heavy American pressure. The cession caused divisions among the western tribes, alienated many who had previously counted the Americans as friends, and strengthened opposition to American expansion.

Americans were not only hostile to traditional native cultures and the old trading economy, but to the foreign powers that threatened to channel Indian discontent over

American encroachment into useful alliance. To the north, the British in Canada presented bitter reminders of the way in which the British had used Indian auxiliaries in the American Revolution. Towards the Gulf Coast, Spanish Florida cooperated with trading companies with ties to ex-loyalists who provided an avenue for British trade goods into southern Indian villages.

Meanwhile, Indian peoples were faced with hard choices. After decades of brutal warfare which had shattered economic life and political cohesion, many Shawnee began to move once more. Others, like those led by Black Hoof, worked toward accommodating the new economic and political American order which had taken root all around them. Still others, disgusted with the Fort Wayne cession (1809) and led by the inspired vision of Tenskwatawa, the Shawnee Prophet, came to think another way was possible. Tenskwatawa's vision was powerful, attracting adherents from neighboring Algonquian tribes, including Delaware and Miami Indians. Calling for cultural revitalization, the Shawnee Prophet sought to turn his people from the downward spiral of debt caused by declining resources. He called for his people to shun excess, revert to self-sufficiency, and recapture their sacred and powerful connection to their land. Along with his brother Tecumseh, a charismatic military leader, he envisioned Indian people embracing their own cultural values and coming together to thwart efforts by outsiders to determine the tribes' destiny. And, although Tecumseh at first urged peace among tribes, his meaning was clear: Indians must unite and fight to save their lands if necessary. Drawn by the Prophet's powerful vision, nearly one thousand people came to inhabit the multiethnic settlement dedicated to Indian self-sufficiency and unity at Prophet's Town, at the junction of the Wabash and Tippecanoe rivers in Indiana Territory.

Governor William Henry Harrison's move against Prophet's Town was an attempt to thwart the growing movement. But the Shawnees struck first in the early morning hours of November 11, 1811, against the American force that camped near their town. The Americans repulsed the attack and went on to loot and burn the town. Thinking they had carried the day, the Americans claimed the Battle at Tippecanoe a victory. Rather, it resulted in a self-fulfilling prophecy as the survivors turned to the British for aid and the Indian conflict soon merged into America's war with Britain.

As the battle in the north raged, Tecumseh was heading home from a southern tour in which he sought to enlist

Tecumseh warned territorial governor William Henry Harrison that the Treaty of Fort Wayne was invalid. The Indian signers, Tecumseh claimed in his speech (opposite), had no authority to sell land "held in common with other Native peoples."

Although William Henry Harrison repulsed Tenskwatawa's attack at the Battle of Tippecanoe and burned nearby Prophet's Town in 1811, the resurgent Indian confederacy retaliated against the Americans in 1812.

allies in the Shawnee confederation. He found support among the Creeks. There, the National Council had repeatedly given in to demands by the American agent Benjamin Hawkins, including pressure to adopt the civilization program and cede land to the United States. At the meeting that Tecumseh attended, Hawkins asserted that US citizens had the right to travel freely through Creek lands by land and water and vowed that the United States would improve the Federal Road which already ran through Creek territory whether the Council assented to the move or not. Hawkins determined the payment for this "right": 1,500 spinning wheels and the right of an elite few to collect tolls at certain points along the route. Those who opposed these developments were receptive to Tecumseh's warnings about American encroachments on both land and Indian self-determination as well as the call to spiritual renewal espoused by the Prophet. They attempted to harness this spiritual power by performing

the Shawnee dances and undertaking rigorous ceremonies, including self-induced trances.

As Shawnees in the north launched a retaliatory campaign in the spring and summer of 1812 for the destruction of Prophet's Town, the Creek National Council moved against their own people who had attacked settlers on the frontier. Those who robbed or killed travelers and American settlers on the frontier were publicly whipped and executed. The actions, which violated the traditional prerogatives of clan leaders, brought the nation to civil war by the summer of 1813. And in late July, a party of Creek dissidents, known as Red Sticks because they had raised the "red stick" or "red club" of war against their chiefs, was attacked by Mississippi Territorial militia as they returned to their towns from Spanish Pensacola, where they had obtained supplies and ammunition from the Spanish. The Red Sticks retaliated by attacking the fortified plantation of Samuel Mims, where American militia and settlers, many of Creek descent, had gathered for protection, anticipating a Creek attack. The stunning success of the Red Sticks, played up in the national press as a barbarous attack against Americans, brought the United States into the war. Thus, the Creek civil war became a war of American conquest. The war ended with a decisive victory by Andrew Jackson at Horseshoe Bend in late March 1814. By the end of the war, the majority of Upper Creek people were homeless and an estimated half of the population was either dead or seeking refuge in Spanish territory.

By the time Jackson had "humbled" the Creeks, the war in the northwest had largely ended. The battle at Prophet's Town accomplished what Americans had feared: an Indian-British alliance. Indeed, the action against the settlement seemed to confirm Tecumseh's warnings and brought many into his camp. Those warriors who flocked to Tecumseh's resistance movement were armed by and actively supported the British, bringing needed manpower to the Canadian front. More importantly, Tecumseh's warriors were employed to harass American supply lines and threaten American posts, two of which were abandoned (Detroit and Fort Dearborn). In return, Americans took the war to the Indian country, burning Indian villages and fields and leaving civilians homeless and hungry. The bloody frontier battles, in which Tecumseh's followers fought against both American regulars and militia, came to an end on Canadian soil at the Battle of Thames, in October 1813, with the defeat of the British and the death of Tecumseh.

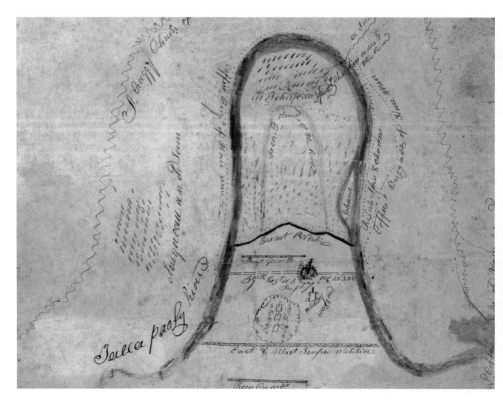

Indian agent Leonard Tarrant drew this map (top) showing the Creek encampment at Tohopeka and the battle lines before the Battle of Horseshoe Bend.

Menawa, a leader of the Red Sticks at the Battle of Horseshoe Bend, continued to oppose American encroachments on Creek land. In 1825, he led the party that carried out the National Council's order to execute Taskanugi Hatke (William McIntosh) for ceding Creek land.

The Treaty of Ghent ended the official war. The British negotiators initially demanded a consideration of Indian boundaries, but soon dropped the issue, leaving negotiations with Indian tribes to the Americans. Thus, it was Jackson's harsh treaty with the Upper Creeks at Fort Jackson in 1814 and the Treaty at Greenville, negotiated a month earlier by William Henry Harrison with the northwestern tribes, that ended the wars for the control of the west. Victories against Indians gave Americans plenty of reasons to believe they had won "the war," for by these treaties, they acquired millions of acres of Indian territory. Andrew Jackson and William Henry Harrison were the heroes of the age, for they had turned back the British threat, secured American borders, opened up vast tracts of Indian lands for settlement, and although they failed to "exterminate" the Indians, left them so weakened that renewed military challenges by an intertribal confederation were all but impossible.

*A professor of history at Auburn University, Kathryn Braund is the editor and contributor to* Tohopeka: Rethinking the Creek War and War of 1812 *(Tuscaloosa: University of Alabama Press, 2012) and is writing a book on the Red Stick War.*

UNITED STATES     KENTUCKY

○ Nashville

*Duck*

TENNESSEE

*Tennessee*

● *Fort Deposit*

*Fort Strother* ●

● Tallushatchee

*Coosa*

Talladega ●

*Enitachopco*

*Fort Williams* ●

Emuckfau

GEORGIA

Battle of Tohopeka/
Horseshoe Bend

*Fort Jackson* ●

*Tallapoosa*

● *Fort
Mitchell*

MISSISSIPPI
TERRITORY

Econochaca
(Holy Ground)

*Alabama*

*Apalachicola*

UISIANA

○ Natchez

Burnt Corn

*Fort
Stoddert* ●

*Fort Mims*

WEST FLORIDA

ADMINISTERED
BY SPAIN

EAST
FLORIDA

Baton
Rouge ○

*Lake
Pontchartrain*

Mobile ●

*Cat
Island*

*Mobile
Bay*

*Fort
Bowyer*

★ Pensacola

New Orleans

*Pea
Island*

Battle of New Orleans
Chalmette

*Fort
Saint Philip*

GULF OF
MEXICO

North
⬆

0      100      200 Kilometers

0      100      200 Miles

✺ War of 1812 battle/skirmish
● United States fort
● American Indian village
○ United States or British settlement

The shifting iconography (counter-clockwise, from top left) of the Battle of the Thames and the death of Tecumseh in many ways paralleled the political career of Richard Johnson. The first image, created shortly after the battle, shows no direct combat between Johnson (mounted) and Tecumseh (with spear in hand).

Elected to Congress in 1829, Johnson moved into the battle foreground in an 1830s battle image. By the 1840s, an image by Nathaniel Currier elevated Vice President Johnson to center stage, now unquestionably a warrior hero in a battle reduced to the killing of Tecumseh.

Over many decades, one artist after another imagined the dramatic, final moments of the life of Shawnee warrior Tecumseh. Popular images like the lithograph by Nathaniel Currier (below) graced antebellum parlors. With chaotic battle all around, a heroic American officer confronts and vanquishes a romanticized Indian adversary.

Beyond the details and the accuracy of the scene depicted—they still are debated 200 years later—in retrospect we do know that on October 5, 1813, Tecumseh's single-minded mission, a secure Indian homeland, died with him in Ontario, Canada, at the Battle of the Thames. Each "Death of Tecumseh" image allegorically, intended or not, captured not just the last moments of the warrior's life but also the demise of his dream.

Ironically, the same moment in time also symbolized an alternative vision. Colonel Richard M. Johnson, the man who took credit for killing Tecumseh, built a political career on his disputed accomplishment. More than two decades after the war, the colonel became the ninth vice president of the United States aided by the memorable and irreverent slogan, "Rumpsey Dumpsey, Rumpsey Dumpsey, Colonel Johnson killed Tecumseh."

# Madison, Party Politics, and the War of 1812

By Andrew Burstein and Nancy Isenberg

*It was known as Mr. Madison's War. Throughout his career James Madison was appreciated for his deliberative character, his leading role in state and national legislatures, and his reasoned opinions on such issues as commerce and constitutions. But no one looked to the guarded, if good-humored, fourth president for wartime leadership.*

Unlike his Princeton contemporaries Colonel Aaron Burr and General Henry "Light-Horse Harry" Lee (the father of Robert E. Lee), he was not a man of action and had never been eager to enter the field of battle. Slight of build, sickly and short, he was nicknamed "Little Madison," and to those who willfully mocked him, "Little Jemmy." Even after having served for eight years as Thomas Jefferson's secretary of state, respectful and sympathetic members of his own Republican Party suspected that President Madison was not temperamentally equipped to lead the nation through a second war with Great Britain.

In 1809, as Madison succeeded Jefferson, the Republicans (also known as Democratic-Republicans) were in the ascendant. Much had changed in twenty years. When George Washington took the oath of office in 1789, formal political parties did not yet exist. Supporters of the new, relatively strong central government were Federalists; those who remained suspicious of centralized power and pressed for a Bill of Rights to explicitly protect individuals against federal encroachment were Antifederalists. But these designations indicated ideological differences, not regular organizations.

During Washington's first term, however, Madison and Jefferson saw danger to the republic in Treasury Secretary Alexander Hamilton's power-engrossing measures. The two Virginians feared an executive who would come to

**Before assuming the presidency, Madison warned of the hazards of warfare. "Of all the enemies to public liberty," he argued, "war is perhaps the most to be dreaded." After inauguration, war dragged him into its feared abyss.**

This British cartoon depicted a United States in chaos. Napoleon and the devil seem to be goading a tormented President Madison into the insanity of war with Great Britain.

imitate the British government and sacrifice republican principles. Despite Madison's crucial work in defining the federalist system in 1787–1788, he, along with Jefferson and others, absorbed former Antifederalists and critics of the administration into what became the Republican Party. Washington administration stalwarts retained the name Federalists; their last successful presidential nominee was John Adams, and they would be politically defunct by 1815. In Andrew Jackson's time, the Jeffersonian-Madisonian Republicans were known as Democrats, and are thus ancestors of today's Democratic Party—not the Republican Party formed in 1856, to which Abraham Lincoln belonged.

The Federalists did not go down easily. From the moment Madison succeeded Jefferson, they were public in their denunciations of the new Republican president. And in the run-up to war, as Madison sought reelection, the opposition *Alexandria [Va.] Gazette* published a nasty piece of doggerel: "Who will be the next President causes great doubt, / As all parties agree whiffling Jemmy goes out." In the vocabulary of the day, to whiffle was to waver. As the saying goes, though, one should not judge a book by its cover. Yes, Madison was a bookworm; but he was also an ardent nationalist keen on American expansion and confident in his ability to conduct the coming war. He was not a whiffler.

In 1810, midway through his first term, Madison had turned his attention to the Gulf of Mexico, deftly managing the acquisition of West Florida from Spain, while making it known that he was interested in annexing East Florida as well when that became feasible. Spain was militarily weak, unlike England. Madison dreamed of incorporating Canada as well as Spanish Cuba into the expanding Union, but the United States was not strong enough to advance its aims through bluster and the fiscally conservative Republican president was initially unprepared to spend adequately on national defense.

Instead, he looked for ways to pressure London to back down from its bullying on the high seas. The 1807 Orders-in-Council, which threatened all neutral shipping, had not been rescinded. Early in his presidency, Madison assured his predecessor that he would stand strong, with "a prudent adherence to our essential interests." By April 1812, he had determined that the British "prefer war with us, to a repeal of their Orders-in-Council. We have nothing left therefore, but to make ready for it." The retired Jefferson thoroughly concurred.

In the march to war, the administration worried about political resistance in Federalist New England. Madison saw "intrigue" and "seditious opposition" in those who "clogged the wheels of war." He could not rely on Federalist-dominated states to provide able-bodied men for military service.

In Swiss-born Pennsylvanian Albert Gallatin, Madison had a very dependable and highly competent advisor. He had initially wanted Gallatin for secretary of state, but his foreign birth and French accent had, since the early 1790s, provoked a backlash from Federalists, who regarded Gallatin as insufficiently American. Now, twenty years later, he still made the Federalists uncomfortable, and so, rather than add to the already poisoned political atmosphere, the president retained Gallatin in the same cabinet office he had held under Jefferson: secretary of the treasury. The man he appointed secretary of state, Robert Smith of Maryland, was a Princetonian like himself, but one who hated Gallatin and, as things turned out, felt no loyalty to Madison either. For as long as Smith remained at State, the president would be poorly served.

Madison had been the dominant voice in Congress in the formative decade of the 1790s, and a virtual "co-president" with Jefferson from 1801 to 1809. But in his own first term,

The government saved money during the tenure of Secretary of the Treasury Albert Gallatin by mothballing the navy and keeping the army small. Militarily and financially, the United States discovered it was unprepared for war.

he presided over a fractious cabinet. Smith was eventually replaced by James Monroe, who was not just an old friend and a former diplomat (to both England and France), but also an officer during the American Revolution who still aspired to ride at the head of an army. With Gallatin and Monroe at his side after the war began in earnest, Madison would be hearing from experienced and politically savvy men whom he knew he could trust.

Even within his party, though, Madison faced resistance. John Randolph of Roanoke, an outspoken antiwar Virginia congressman, feared spiraling costs, and declared: "Our people will not submit to being taxed." Randolph was outvoted by the War Hawks in Congress (those who supported the war), led by the oratorically powerful Speaker of the House Henry Clay of Kentucky, who, late in 1811, sent Madison a bottle of Madeira in celebration of the president's third annual message to Congress, which addressed the "ominous" indications of belligerency on the part of London. Reacting to a breakdown in negotiations, Madison spoke unabashedly about British intransigence: "With this evidence of hostile inflexibility in trampling on rights which no independent nation can relinquish, Congress will feel the duty of putting the United States into an armor and an attitude demanded by the crisis, and corresponding with the national spirit and expectations." Another Kentuckian and a future vice president, Richard Mentor Johnson, termed President Madison's address a "manly and bold attitude of war."

Madison has received little notice for his forward posture, as history tends to attribute all war fever to the leaders of the House of Representatives. But the president was by no means positioned in the background. Two decades after his death, his private secretary Edward Coles wrote that Madison may have been less "rampant" than the "noisy politicians" who urged war; but after the fighting commenced, he proved himself "less crouching under difficulties" than most of these verbally energetic men. Madison was not just a thinker. He was an assertive politician. A little known incident foreshadowed the onset of formal hostilities, with which the president was intimately connected. One John Henry, an Irishman who had lived in the United States before removing to Canada, sold information to the administration which purported to prove that certain prominent New Englanders, who thrived on trade with London, were in cahoots with the British ministry. Desirous of adding Canada to the United States, believing that war with Great Britain would very possibly make this goal attainable, Madison consented to

*Richard Mentor Johnson termed President Madison's address a "manly and bold attitude of war."*

Elected Speaker of the House of Representatives on the first day of his first session, Henry Clay became the "guiding spirit" of the War Hawks, appointing political allies to chair important House committees.

# First Blood: Baltimore Riots

The first casualties of the war occurred on the streets of Baltimore not the battlefield.

Before and during the War of 1812, newspapers and printers played a central role in politics. Openly partisan, they minced few words in supporting candidates and policies. On and off for years, publishers provoked backlash with inflammatory rhetoric. In 1798, for example, a Philadelphia mob threatened the home and office of printer Benjamin Franklin Bache, Benjamin Franklin's outspoken grandson.

The riots that occurred in Baltimore in 1812, just days after the June 18 declaration of war, not only continued the tradition of mobs in the streets but elevated verbal conflict beyond physical violence to murder.

Supporters of the war labeled opposition as treason, and the publisher of the *Federal Republican* newspaper, Alexander Contee Hanson, gave them plenty to condemn. Hanson viewed Baltimore's Democratic-Republicans as "mostly European rabble out to pervert the true principles of the Constitution." He embraced a straightforward goal—"attack the administration in any and every way; show that the Jeffersonians had sold out to France and were supporting Napoleon. "The last hope of civilization, law, and order," Hanson wrote, "was old Mother England."

A mob took the verbal bait, attacked, and destroyed Hanson's office. When the paper reopened, defenders fired into another mob and killed two. After surrendering, Hanson and his supporters were hauled from jail and beaten. Revolutionary War veterans Henry "Light-Horse Harry" Lee, father of five-year-old Robert E. Lee, and James Lingan both received crippling injuries; Lingan died from his wounds.

**This political cartoon is filled with symbolism that readers of the day understood. A 19th-century history of Maryland by John Thomas Sharf, printed decades after the event, still opened with a multipage, detailed account of the attack on the *Federal Republican* office, the victims of the attack, and the aftermath.**

**With historical accounts in hand, scholars can decipher some of the cartoon. Clues suggest the identities of several figures. Alexander Contee Hanson is the horned devil. Hanson supporters include Robert Goodloe Harper, holding the harp. Richard Crabb has a crab in his hat, and Charles Kilgour holds a bull's head suggesting bull-headed insistence on publishing antiwar sentiments. The dancers with tomahawks surely include antiwar Federalist "Light-Horse Harry" Lee.**

pay Henry the then outrageous sum of $50,000. A threat of disunion—an espionage caper originating in Canada— would be enough to justify a northern invasion. If true, the Henry material, along with British-inspired Indian attacks in America's northwest, would mean that Canada was no longer a passive country. As US troops pushed north, the border would dissolve. As it turned out, however, John Henry's papers contained no "smoking gun," no actual names of Federalist conspirators. The US Treasury was drained of $50,000, which it could ill afford, yet the buildup to war did not abate.

On June 1, 1812, Madison came forward with a definitive list of unredressed grievances against Great Britain. These included impressment of US seamen on the Atlantic (forcing sailors to serve aboard British warships), the despised Orders-in-Council, and incitement of Indians against frontier positions. The House Foreign Affairs Committee met and agreed that London's hypocrisies could no longer be tolerated. The long period of anxious anticipation ended, as both houses of Congress voted for war that same month. The tally was 79 to 49 in the House, 19 to 13 in the Senate (some days later, and only after extended debate).

It was not a war for which enthusiasm could be retained long. The only obvious cause in the minds of most people was the British insult to America's honor. According to Federalist New England, Madison had fabricated a threat of invasion when none existed; he was prepared only for a "Quixotic expedition" into Canada, on the basis of flimsy evidence that the nation was even under attack. London, the Federalists said, was eager to resolve differences and would modify its position on impressment—that insult to America's honor. This was, in fact, partly true. The British wanted to avert a war with the United States. The Orders-in-Council were to be repealed. Had the administration waited a little longer, the expensive war might have been averted.

Not all Federalists lived in the North. Those south of the Mason-Dixon line noted that the war would reverse Secretary Gallatin's good work in pointing the United States toward a balanced budget and retirement of the national debt. The War Hawks, bent on reclaiming honor, yet staunchly opposed to taxes, seemed strangely unconcerned about the road they were taking. The Federalists had not won the presidency since John Adams had faced Thomas Jefferson in 1796. If enough Americans were killed in combat, they figured, they could replace Madison with one of their own.

Then as now, political satirists spared the sensibilities of few politicians. This 1814 drawing pilloried members of the Hartford Convention. George III promises his "Yankey boys" "plenty of molasses and Codfish; plenty of goods to Smuggle; Honours, titles and Nobility." Federalist Timothy Pickering, secretary of state under George Washington and John Adams, is on his knees praying for a fictitious lordship as Massachusetts drags "poor little" Rhode Island and reluctant Connecticut toward the cliff of secession.

O'tis my Yankey boys! jump in my fine fellows; plenty molasses and Codfish; plenty of goods to Smuggle; Honours, titles and Nobility into the bargain —

Wm Charles, Sr.

NO *LEAP.*

One of the very dangers that James Madison warned against when he wrote in support of the US Constitution haunted his presidency. "The influence of factious leaders may kindle a flame within their particular States," Madison wrote in Federalist #10, "but will be unable to spread a general conflagration through the other States."

Madison's own political supporters in the south and west avidly kindled such a "flame" when they loudly and persistently pushed the government toward war, citing British infringements on shipping, damage to international prestige, and Indian attacks on the frontier.

The Federalist Party, on the other hand, still strong in several New England states, thought that war with Great Britain would prove to be costly and damage commerce. They not only opposed war but discouraged enlistments and war funding. Sure enough, after several years of lax enforcement in New England, the British tightened their blockade, occupied the territory of Maine, and invaded the Champlain Valley.

In response to war costs levied by the federal government, 26 delegates from Massachusetts, Connecticut, Rhode Island, New Hampshire, and Vermont met at Hartford, Connecticut, in late 1814. These "secessionists" were convinced that New England had a "duty" to assert its authority over unconstitutional infringements on its sovereignty, though the official convention proceedings revealed a relatively moderate stance.

Bad timing doomed the Hartford Convention. Just as the commissioners formalized their demands, the war ended, forever tainting the convention and the Federalist Party with accusations of disunion and treason.

Was Madison correct after all? Could a well-designed republic control the spread of factions and avoid a "general conflagration"?

It had been the Republicans' routine to geographically balance the ticket: a Virginia president accepted a New Yorker as his running mate. But in April 1812, Vice President George Clinton died in office. His nephew, DeWitt Clinton, decided to challenge the incumbent, rallying two unlikely constituencies: Republicans in Congress who were not keen on the war, and Federalists who could be convinced that they had no national base left and would be better served by electing the putative Republican Clinton—at least he was not a southerner, and he could be reasoned with.

The presidential election that took place in the fall of 1812 was a referendum on the war. Madison was in his sixtieth year and Clinton, forty-three, was brimming with confidence and working hard at cementing a coalition of fellow New Yorkers and disaffected New Englanders. In the end, however, populous Pennsylvania went for Madison and the solid South returned him to office. Clinton had won seven of the eighteen states, but none south of Delaware. The Republicans turned to Elbridge Gerry of Massachusetts as vice president. Though Gerry and Madison had experienced moments of contention at the Constitutional Convention, they were politically compatible these many years later.

As a reminder of the uncertainties in national politics in this first year of a renewed fight with Great Britain, War Hawk Henry Clay confided to Caesar Rodney, who had resigned as Attorney General of the United States some months before war was declared: "Mr. Madison is wholly unfit for the storms of war." And storms he would face.

As Madison began his second term in the spring of 1813, Secretary Gallatin warned him: "We hardly have enough money to last till the end of the month." On the ground, the Americans did not perform well either. The early effort to drive into Canada, through Detroit, turned into a rout. Michigan's territorial governor, William Hull, a colonel in the Revolution, failed miserably. Monroe called him "weak, indecisive, and pusillanimous," while hopeful that the embarrassment would "rouse the nation" and ultimately lead to victory. He was echoing the president's position when he said: "We must efface the stain before we make peace, & that may give us Canada."

The United States saw better prospects on the water. Naval commanders proved indefatigable and aggressive; the most

First lady Dolley Madison not only proved her mettle during the British attack on Washington, DC, but also served as President Madison's political partner, bolstering his resolve during the most difficult years of the war.

celebrated, Stephen Decatur, ranged farthest. He fought and defeated a British frigate east of the Canary Islands and brought it home as a prize of war; a lieutenant showed up in Washington, DC, and laid its flag at the feet of first lady Dolley Madison.

Within Madison's cabinet, an ineffective secretary of the navy was replaced with a former ship's captain, William Jones, who encouraged privateers to harass British vessels. Jones organized a massive shipbuilding effort on the shores of Lakes Erie and Ontario. Madison strongly favored an enlarged navy, and he recognized that he would have to adjust Republican cost-saving measures in order to accomplish this end. Ironically, in order to prosecute the war more fully, the Madison administration adopted a number of policies earlier championed by the Federalists such as investing in bigger and better ships, re-chartering the National Bank, and increasing the national debt.

Even so, by the time of the British attack on Washington in August 1814, when the President's House (now the White House) and the Capitol were both put to the torch, the nation no longer understood what the war was meant to accomplish. Canada was not to be taken. Little, indeed, was to be gained. In Europe, American negotiators John Quincy Adams, Albert Gallatin, and yes, the War Hawk Henry Clay, fought tooth and nail to secure a just peace along with a return to *status quo ante bellum* (the state that existed before the war). The treaty signed on December 24, 1814, was, in effect, an indefinite end to an indefinite war.

Andrew Jackson's sensational victory at the Battle of New Orleans on January 8, 1815, before the Treaty of Ghent was received in Washington, proved to be a particular point of pride. President Madison reaped unexpected benefits from the final outcome. "The tools of royalty have never ceased prating against the imbecility and weakness of republics," a Rhode Island newspaper proclaimed. "Where are these false prophets now? The republic is safe." The president allowed publication of a semiofficial white paper, which he coauthored with Pennsylvanian Alexander James Dallas, his new secretary of the treasury and a close ally of Gallatin's. It justified the administration's actions, step by step, and indicted the British for barbarism.

The president, historically portrayed as mild and modest, and never known for defending himself before posterity, was intent on having the public record reflect the correctness of his course as commander-in-chief. He did not possess the eloquence of his friend Jefferson, but one Pennsylvania senator, who spent a good deal of time in his company in the gloomy year of 1814, said of him that he remained cheerful, despite the trials of war, maintaining the composure that "ever became a great man."

To us, a slightly different picture emerges: James Madison exhibited open-mindedness when many around him held petty, rigid views. A man who never once left American shores in his eighty-five years, he knew his limitations when it came to military planning. He was, then, a quintessentially practical man who enlisted the advice of seasoned soldiers, proving himself in the end a war president who understood power, reacted with composure to the hostility of his domestic enemies, and saved face.

*Andrew Burstein and Nancy Isenberg are professors of history at Louisiana State University and coauthors of* Madison and Jefferson *(New York: Random House, 2010).*

Despite the humiliation of the British attack on Washington, DC, the war resulted in no exchange of territory but left historians considerable fodder for the ongoing debate over winners and losers.

# "The Luxuriant Shoots of Our Tree of Liberty": American Maritime Experience in the War of 1812

By Paul A. Gilje

*Thomas Jefferson was never more wrong. In late June 1812 he wrote to his friend Thaddeus Kosciuszko that no war had been "entered into under more favorable auspices" and that "[o]ur present enemy will have the seas to herself, while we shall be equally predominant at land, and shall strip her of all her possessions on this continent." The American army quickly experienced a series of horrendous reverses, while the navy gained triumph after triumph in exploits that proved an important tonic for the pride of the United States.*

On August 13, 1812, Captain David Porter's frigate the *Essex* captured the smaller *Alert*, the first British ship to surrender to the Americans in the war. Under Captain Isaac Hull the *Constitution* gained fame before even fighting a battle by escaping the clutches of several British ships off New York Harbor in July when, in an act of seamanship and fortitude, the ship outran the British in a calm by using kedge anchors (the ship's boats rowed the anchors in front of the *Constitution* and then used the capstan to crank the ship forward) to keep ahead of the pursuit. When a gust of wind finally appeared the *Constitution* got clean away. Once at sea, the *Constitution* defeated the *Guerriere* on August 19, 1812, pounding the smaller and outmanned frigate so badly it had to be sunk. It was in this battle that the *Constitution* earned its nickname "Old Ironsides" because the strength of the oak on the sides of the ship hardly gave way when struck by the *Guerriere*'s shot. The record of the American "super

Martyl Schweig's mural in the Recorder of Deeds Building in Washington, DC, commemorates the contributions of African American sailors, particularly Cyrus Tiffany, during the War of 1812.

Popular celebrations of naval victories, like these lusterware ceramic pitchers from Philadelphia, underscored the symbolic importance of the US Navy's triumphs while the nation suffered a series of defeats on land during the early years of the war.

frigates" continued when the *United States*, under captain Stephen Decatur, captured the *Macedonian* on October 25, 1812, bringing its battered prize safely back to New York. The *Constitution*, under the command of William Bainbridge, destroyed the *Java* in a fierce battle in the South Atlantic on December 29, 1812. Astounded by these defeats, the British Admiralty ordered its captains to avoid single ship actions and proclaimed that battles against the super frigates were not even contests.

The Royal Navy was right, the victories of the *Constitution* and the *United States* were unequal contests. The American super frigates were the top of their class. Designed in the 1790s originally to deal with the Algerian crisis in 1794, they were as fast as any ship afloat, had more firepower, and carried more men than the average British frigate. They were so big that in the right conditions they might have been a match for the smallest of the first-rate British ships (more than 64 guns), although they were dwarfed by the bigger ships of the line carrying upwards of 100 guns. But there were only six super frigates at the beginning of the war. The rest of the navy was comprised of smaller frigates like the *Essex*, which was almost half the tonnage of the *Constitution*, or brigs and sloops of war of even lesser size.

American triumphs occurred with these smaller ships as well. On October 18, 1812, the 18-gun sloop *Wasp* had the effrontery to attack a British convoy and then captured the 22-gun *Frolic*. Unfortunately for the Americans, no sooner had the *Wasp* beaten the larger British vessel, than a 74-gun British ship appeared, forcing the hobbled *Wasp*—its rigging was in shambles from the battle—to surrender. The Americans scored another victory on February 24, 1813, when the brig *Hornet* met the *Peacock* off the coast of South America. The battle was short and brutal. Although the vessels were about the same size, the *Hornet* had more firepower, was better handled, and had more effective gunnery. In a matter of minutes, the *Hornet* so overwhelmed the *Peacock*, that it soon sank. (The *Hornet* would also beat another vessel of equal size, the *Penguin*, in the South Atlantic on March 23, 1815.)

There were also some defeats. The British gained an important symbolic victory when the *Shannon* defeated the *Chesapeake* on June 1, 1813, in a battle off Boston in which Captain James Lawrence uttered the famous words "Don't give up the ship" shortly before the Americans had to haul down their colors after the loss of over a third of the crew.

Many of these battles assumed the aura of a duel between two knights-errant as officers in the American and British navies believed in a code of honor in combat that prized manliness and duty. Captain Lawrence, for example, could have avoided his loss, and the bloodshed that accompanied it, had he remained focused more on what damage they might do to enemy commerce than glory in a ship-to-ship engagement. Likewise, British captains early in the war did not shy away from fighting the American super frigates, like the *United States* and the *Constitution*. The public in both nations eagerly sought word of these confrontations and romanticized the exploits of their hero officers, regardless of the gruesome reality of battles at sea. They also trumpeted the common seamen who manned these ships as defenders of the nation. If each side lionized the captains and their crews, they demonized the enemy. When word arrived in London of the capture of Captain Porter, whom the British newspapers had proclaimed a buccaneer, Parliament cheered. Every time an American naval vessel returned to port with some claim to fame, churches rang their bells, guns fired salutes, and the people in the street celebrated their heroes with a parade.

If the ocean-going navy buoyed American confidence and patriotism with its victories in salt water, the navy's

*Many [naval] battles assumed the aura of a duel between two knights-errant...*

Following his success aboard USS *Hornet*, Captain James Lawrence took command of USS *Chesapeake*. During a fierce sea battle with HMS *Shannon*, Lawrence fell mortally wounded, uttering his famous order, "Don't give up the ship," before being carried below deck.

performance on fresh water altered the outcome of the war. The Great Lakes were vital arteries to transport men and supplies for the armies of the time. Neither side could prosecute a major land invasion without first securing one or more of the Great Lakes.

On a number of occasions, the British under Sir James Yeo and Americans under Isaac Chauncey maneuvered for position on Lake Ontario, fired upon one another, and seemed poised to fight. But in each instance, one or the other pulled back, believing his opponent had an advantage. This stalemate, along with victories on Lake Erie and Lake Champlain, ensured that the United States would not lose any territory as a result of the army's bungling.

After the American surrender of Detroit by General William Hull on August 16, 1812, the British dominated all of Michigan and the upper Great Lakes. The only way to drive the British back was to control Lake Erie. Throughout the summer of 1813, two young energetic naval commanders led a furious effort on each side to build and man a fleet of ships. Lieutenant Robert Barclay of the Royal Navy initially had the advantage, but by early September he had a smaller fleet with fewer men and resources. Unable to convince his superiors to send him men and additional guns, he stripped Fort Malden of its cannon for his squadron. Lieutenant Oliver Hazard Perry in the meanwhile had amassed a fleet of ten ships to meet Barclay. In a hotly contested battle at Put-in-Bay on the western edge of the lake, the two squadrons met on September 10, 1813. Perry's flagship, named after the "martyred" Captain James Lawrence, used Lawrence's famous words "Don't give up the ship" as a banner at its masthead. Perry, however, had to give up the *Lawrence* after it was disabled, and transferred his flag to the *Niagara*. Though the *Lawrence* had been severely battered, the British ships were in worse shape. Perry sailed the relatively unharmed *Niagara* straight into the British line, captured the British flagship, and compelled the rest of the British ships to surrender. Each side had about 500 men at the beginning of the battle. By the time the British hauled down their colors, Barclay had lost 135 killed and wounded (including a seriously injured Barclay); Perry had 123 casualties. In a memorable use of combat rhetoric, Perry sent a short message to General William Henry Harrison—"We have met the enemy and they are ours"—words repeated in history books ever since. In the aftermath of the battle, Harrison was able to recapture Detroit and secure a foothold in Canada.

Previous page: Its oak hull earned USS *Constitution* the nickname "Old Ironsides," shown here engaged with HMS *Guerriere*. The poem "Old Ironsides," by Oliver Wendell Holmes Sr., helped save *Constitution*, now the oldest commissioned ship afloat.

Commodore Oliver Hazard Perry (bottom left) honored his friend James Lawrence by adopting "Dont give up the ship" on the battle pennant of his flagship US Brig *Lawrence* (bottom right). Perry transported the banner and command of his embattled squadron from the battered *Lawrence* to US Brig *Niagara* and sailed to victory in the contest for the Great Lakes. William Henry Powell later distilled Perry's victory in the Battle of Lake Erie into a romanticized rowboat tableau (top).

A second great battle was on Lake Champlain in the waning moments of the war. The British launched a major invasion of upstate New York that would have easily overwhelmed the American land forces if they could defeat the navy on Lake Champlain. While the British began their assault on Plattsburgh, nearly equal squadrons fought on the lake. The American commander, Thomas Macdonough, had anchored his ships in Plattsburgh Bay with springs to allow the vessels to swirl around and use fresh broadsides when the guns on one side became disabled. At the beginning of the battle, the British had the initial advantage with their long guns, but as they closed the American carronades took their toll. After Macdonough's flagship, the *Saratoga*, swung around and brought its fresh guns into the fray, the British flagship, *Confiance*, attempted to mimic the maneuver. The British ship's rigging ran afoul. In the confusion it suffered such damage that the crew refused to fight. Two other British ships surrendered in the battle. The American triumph was complete despite heavy losses: the British had at least 270 killed and wounded and about 200 captured; Macdonough lost 54 men killed and 57 wounded out of 800 men. With the Americans in control of the lake, the British army retreated to Canada in an operation that became an embarrassment to Great Britain.

Americans had reason to cheer the officers and crews of their navy. Although there had been a Continental Navy during the Revolutionary War, the US government had sold its last ship during the 1780s and did not create a new navy until 1794. Once the Algerian crisis had been settled, the construction of three super frigates was suspended, while three others slowly crept toward completion. The United States, however, was also caught in the middle of the conflict between Great Britain and France that erupted in 1793 and would continue with some interruptions until 1815. Being neutral in a world at war was not easy. In 1794 the United States faced a crisis with Great Britain that was settled by the Jay Treaty. The French viewed this agreement, in which the Americans accepted British definitions of contraband to obtain some commercial rights to trade with Great Britain, as a violation of the 1778 Franco-American alliance. Having come to the aid of the Americans during the Revolutionary War, the French were outraged by the American willingness to come to terms with the British. The French began to seize American shipping leading to the Quasi-War (1797–1800). In response the United States began a rapid naval build up, completed all six super frigates, and purchased and constructed other vessels bringing the navy to a total of

33 ships. The navy depended upon a pool of officers and sailors who gained experience in the expanding merchant marine. The Quasi-War, which included several naval victories, enhanced that experience. Jefferson wanted to shrink the navy once he became president in 1801 and rely on gunboats for coastal defense. However, a war with Tripoli meant keeping several frigates and other ships on active duty in the Mediterranean as nursery for sailors and a new crop of officers, including men like Stephen Decatur, whose seamanship, dashing, and bravery won them fame and promotion. In the process the navy established a tradition of excellence.

Motivation mattered. The British navy, too, had seasoned captains and crews, and they had centuries of experience in designing and building warships. But the Americans had an intangible asset. Samuel Leech, who had served on the *Macedonian* when it fought the *United States* and later served in the American navy, acknowledged that the American super frigate had an advantage in size, guns, and men. But he also believed that the seamen "in the two ships fought under the influence of different motives." Leech briefly traced the history of impressment—the forced recruitment of sailors into the British navy. This practice,

Many of the naval heroes of the War of 1812, celebrated in this mid-19th century Currier print, received valuable training and experience during the Tripolitan War a decade earlier under the tutelage of Commodore Edward Preble.

# The War of 1812 at Sea

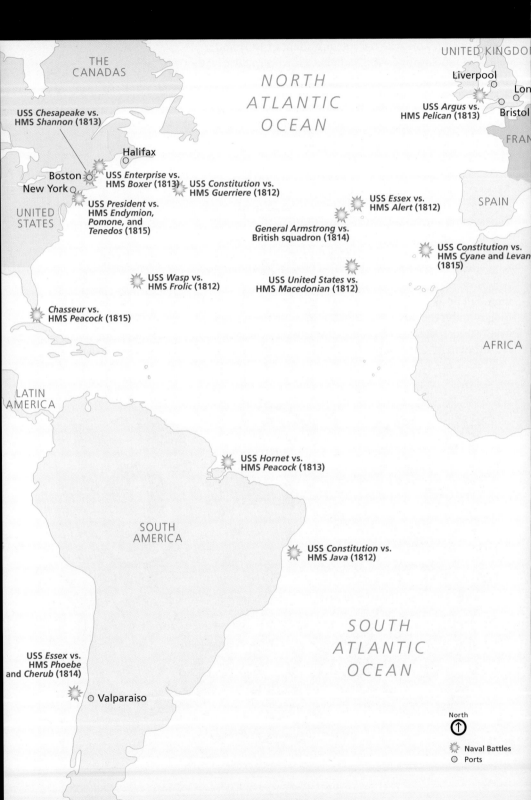

THE CANADAS

NORTH ATLANTIC OCEAN

UNITED KINGDOM

Liverpool

Lon

USS *Argus* vs. HMS *Pelican* (1813)

Bristol

FRAN

USS *Chesapeake* vs. HMS *Shannon* (1813)

Halifax

Boston

New York

USS *Enterprise* vs. HMS *Boxer* (1813)

USS *Constitution* vs. HMS *Guerriere* (1812)

SPAIN

UNITED STATES

USS *President* vs. HMS *Endymion, Pomone,* and *Tenedos* (1815)

USS *Essex* vs. HMS *Alert* (1812)

General Armstrong vs. British squadron (1814)

USS *Constitution* vs. HMS *Cyane* and *Levan* (1815)

USS *Wasp* vs. HMS *Frolic* (1812)

USS *United States* vs. HMS *Macedonian* (1812)

Chasseur vs. HMS *Peacock* (1815)

AFRICA

LATIN AMERICA

USS *Hornet* vs. HMS *Peacock* (1813)

SOUTH AMERICA

USS *Constitution* vs. HMS *Java* (1812)

SOUTH ATLANTIC OCEAN

USS *Essex* vs. HMS *Phoebe* and *Cherub* (1814)

Valparaiso

North

Naval Battles

Ports

which included the taking of thousands of American citizens as well as British subjects, was one of the leading causes of the War of 1812. Many sailors on the *Macedonian* had been swept up by press gangs in ports and on the high seas. Such men might be less than eager to fight. Moreover, some of the sailors on the *Macedonian* were Americans who had been taken from American merchant vessels and who were "inwardly hoping for defeat." In comparison, the men in the United States Navy were volunteers, who received better treatment, and knew that they were fighting for "Free trade and sailors' rights"—an object with which, as Leech explained, "our men could but sympathize, whatever our officers might do."

Sailors, however, could also have more mercenary motives. Prize money served as an important incentive encouraging men to serve at sea. This was true for the regular navy, and was even more significant for the men who signed aboard the more than 500 authorized privateers—privately owned ships commissioned by the government to capture enemy commerce in a form of legalized piracy. Nations used privateers to raid commerce, capture supplies, and injure the enemy's economy. Privateers tended to avoid ship-to-ship battles and were usually fast-sailing schooners and sloops packed with men. Speed enabled the privateer to run down any merchant vessel it came across and to out-sail British naval vessels. Large crews for these smallish ships intimidated merchant vessels into surrendering and they provided manpower for prize crews to take the captured vessel to a friendly port. Privateers often had polyglot crews, which were, as common seaman George Little explained, "composed of all nations; they appeared to have been scraped together from the lowest dens of wretchedness and vice, and only wanted a leader to induce them to any acts of daring and desperation." These ships also had plenty of inexperienced men who were "not making money fast enough" on land and decided to "cruise for dollars, where they were to be found in greater plenty" than in their home towns. Although the British managed to capture many of these ships, privateersmen continued to slip out to sea, exacting a heavy toll on British shipping. In all, privateers damaged the British economy more severely than did the American navy: 23 American navy vessels captured 254 ships; the total privateer haul was 1,345 ships for a net worth of $45.5 million.

Both privateers and American naval vessels had crews which included white and black Americans as well as men from other countries. Some were experienced sailors; others were "green" landsmen. Aboard ship there was a rough

*[American sailors] demonstrated a sense of entitlement that reflected their faith in the rights of men and their belief in a peculiar notion of liberty.*

George Roberts, an African American gunner and privateersman on the brig *Chasseur*, sailed out of Fell's Point, Maryland. Homeport for dozens of privateers, this waterfront community in Baltimore was a target of the Royal Navy.

your Colours you with your Stripes we'll Stripe you!

**A British cartoon mocked the American "special penchant for liberty" by portraying the sailors aboard the USS *Chesapeake* as unruly, undisciplined, and easily subdued by HMS *Shannon*.**

equality among seamen with African Americans living and serving next to European Americans. Ashore, however, racial prejudice persisted. At Dartmoor Prison in England, where as many as 6,000 Americans were detained by the end of the war, white American sailors insisted that the black sailors live in a separate building.

Whether aboard privateers or navy ships, Americans expressed an independent spirit which may have given them an edge in combat. The American tars, as sailors were often called, demonstrated a sense of entitlement that reflected their faith in the rights of men and their belief in a peculiar notion of liberty— a liberty that frequently revealed

itself in unruly behavior that owed as much to a tradition of rowdiness as it did to the democratic ideals of the American Revolution. Ordinarily ships were autocracies, with the captain reigning supreme. On American ships officers often had to follow rather than lead their crews. When the captain on the USS *Syren* died, the lieutenant asked the crew if they wanted to continue the voyage or return to port—the crew voted to stay at sea. Aboard a privateer during the war a captain shortened the rum ration, only to find that his crew refused to work without getting their just share of grog. After two days, and with a squall coming on, the captain "found that his government was democratical" and he "conceded to the large and fearful majority; and the New England spirit carried the day."

This spirit also came to the fore when Americans were held as prisoners of war. The American tar's "wild reckless, daring, enterprizing character" flummoxed British officials who could only exclaim "that it would puzzle the d[evi]l to keep them in good order." Whereas, the American militia and regular military might also be difficult to control, sailors seemed to have a special penchant for liberty. Serving as a surgeon aboard a privateer, Amos G. Babcock came to know and appreciate the common seamen, recognizing that sailors "are full of 'rights' and 'wrongs' of 'justice and injustice,'" and of defining crimes, and asserting "the butts and bounds of national and individual rights." Babcock later explained "the spirit of fun and frolic" that characterized American prisoners of war, and the "provoking" actions against their British captors, as one of "the luxuriant shoots of our tree of liberty" that revealed "the strength, depth, and extent of its roots, and the richness of the soil." American sailor prisoners of war tried the patience of their captives repeatedly until tragedy struck in the Dartmoor Massacre of April 6, 1815—a tragedy in which British guards fired into a crowd of boisterous sailors, killing seven, several months after the war was over. Although "the luxuriant shoots of our tree of liberty" led to tragedy at Dartmoor, the sailors' challenge to British authority bore witness to their commitment to "Free Trade and Sailors' Rights," an ideologically infused motto rooted in the soil of America's revolutionary past and reaffirmed during the War of 1812.

*Paul A. Gilje is George Lynn Cross Research Professor at the University of Oklahoma. He is the author of* Free Trade and Sailors' Rights in the War of 1812 *(New York: Cambridge University Press, 2013).*

# Land Operations in the War of 1812

By David S. Heidler and Jeanne T. Heidler

*On the scale of war as waged in Europe during the age of Napoleon, the War of 1812 was a minor affair. In 1812, as Napoleon was invading Russia with a half million men, the United States on the other side of the world was trying to conquer Canada with forces numbering about one-tenth of a percent of the Grande Armée's size. While individual European battles counted casualties in the tens of thousands, about 6,000 Americans were killed or wounded during the entire War of 1812.*

Americans could count themselves fortunate that the British military was preoccupied with Napoleon for most of the Anglo-American conflict. That good fortune saved the country in the first two years of the fight. Broad disunity and sectional discord in New England made the War of 1812 one of the most bungled military ventures in the Republic's history. Neither the country nor its politicians could agree on the wisdom of challenging Britain, and these deep divisions hobbled the war effort. Pro-war congressmen were sufficiently organized, voluble, and energetic to earn the label War Hawks, but military disasters limited their ability to shape events. Steeped in the tradition of a passive executive, President James Madison was temperamentally unsuited for the demands of wartime leadership. His subordinates were often incompetent placeholders out of touch with the mood of the country, which was divided between apathy and disagreement over the wisdom of the war in the first place, let alone how to prosecute it.

Political dissent coincided with appalling military unpreparedness, a problem evident from the top down. Many ranking generals were aging relics of the Revolutionary War.

*Broad disunity and sectional discord in New England made the War of 1812 one of the most bungled military ventures in the Republic's history.*

Battle art often contains fact and fiction. Romanticized 19th- and early 20th-century images rarely showed the full composition of Jackson's New Orleans army—regulars, militia, Choctaw Indians, and free men of color.

William Hull abandoned a meandering invasion of Upper Canada and wound up surrendering Detroit in August 1812 without firing a shot, placing the entire Old Northwest under British control when the war was only a few weeks old. Also that August, Henry Dearborn, senior major general in charge of the northeast theater from the Niagara River to the New England coast, without a shred of authority signed an armistice with Canada's governor-general, an agreement Madison had to repudiate. James Wilkinson, a self-serving opportunist, quarreled with colleague Maj. Gen. Wade Hampton and superior Secretary of War John Armstrong, dooming the 1813 assault on Montreal.

Although promising officers would emerge toward the end of the conflict, younger generals were often no better than their antiquated counterparts. Early in the war, New York militia general Stephen Van Renssalaer was woefully inexperienced and abashedly resigned after losing the Battle of Queenston in October 1812. His successor, regular army general Alexander Smyth, had a talent for drafting bombastic proclamations but could only manage farcical invasion attempts across the Niagara River before his removal from the service. And Madison put young William Winder in charge of Washington's defense in the summer of 1814 because he was politically important (Maryland governor Levin Winder was his uncle) rather than a sound military choice. Within six weeks the capital was occupied by the British and in flames.

The American regular army was too small for its task, a victim of the country's fear of large standing forces. Last-minute efforts to increase the army yielded fewer than 12,000 men by the time Congress declared war in June 1812, and these paltry numbers were about as incompetently trained as they were incompetently led. They were also widely deployed, compelling the government to rely on state militias, a necessity made seemingly virtuous by the tradition that amateur soldiers could fight just as well as professionals and were better into the bargain because they posed no threat to the Republic. Yet they actually did pose an inadvertent threat, for the militia's capacity to disappoint was a chronic problem, and it was the cause of some fearsome disasters. The short nature of militia enlistments made lengthy and remote campaigns impossible, and the absence of central authority over various state organizations meant a lack of coordination in the campaigns in which militia did participate. Several New England states, Massachusetts among them, refused to call up their militias at the start of the war, and when they did muster

This quaintly illustrated broadside reports the British victory at Queenston Heights, the first major battle of the war. Despite a numerical advantage, the poorly trained, inexperienced Americans failed to gain a foothold in Canada.

# A View of the Northern Expedition in Miniature.

## James War.　Tom Patriot.　John Adams.　John Rogers.

*Kill him Bona, kill him & I'll take Canada.*

*Here comes No. 1. Let me at him Bona, and I'll take him down*

*Kill him Bona, & I'll pay all damages.*

*Let me at him Bona, and I'll blow him to atoms.*

Columbia, Columbia, to glory arise,
Fly quick to the north, make Canada a prize,
While it's none to command, it is your's to obey,
Then all hands make ready to seize on the prey.
We'll repair to the northward, stick close to the lines,
Lest we get too far in those northerly climes,
When the water sets in, to Greenbush we'll retire,
And smoak our long pipes by the side of the fire.

Starvation's the fate of the British empire,
My destructive machine will soon make them expire,
Methinks I will make them come under my thumb,
With my little bark that mounts only one gun,
I will bring them to terms by the force of this measure,
Then we'll go abroad & return home at pleasure,
We'll sail to sweet France, & in ev'ry direction,
And no British tyrant demand our protection.

My name is Taxation—in my introduction,
Some people I vext, o prevent their destruction,
Had I to the place of some others been sitting,
I'd built me a navy to cope with Great Britain.
But now I'm retir'd, sees the states in a bustle,
And all I'm afraid, paid too dear for the whistle,
One caution I'd give you before that I leave you,
I'd send Below to Bona, and borrow a navy.

My first to John Bull no true homage will pay,
Though his orders in council forever should stay;
He talks of a fight for to search for his slaves,
Before I grant that I shall sink in the waves;
He had better be silent and send me no threat,
Lest I catch his fish in my old yankee net,
He builds on the Indians that's now with him join'd,
But if Uncle Sam lives, they will all be Bur-goyn'd.

## BATTLE OF QUEENSTOWN.

BUFFALO, October 20, 1812.

On Tuesday morning last, just before day light, in conformity to previous arrangements, Colonel Solomon Van Rensselaer, aid-de-camp to Gen. Van Rensselaer, at the head of 300 volunteer militia, from the 13th regiment, and Col. Christie, with 300 regular troops, the whole under the immediate command of Col. Van Rensselaer, crossed the river at Lewiston in 17 boats, with the intent to storm the enemy's works on the heights or mountain above Queenston. The militia and regulars moved forward with the greatest intrepidity and gallantry, and carried the enemy's works with but a small loss and possessed themselves of the enemy's battery. In this affair, Col. Van Rensselaer was severely wounded in the leg, thigh & side, and was carried back to the American side of the river. Gen. Brock and his aid, Col. M'Donald, of the British forces, were killed in this engagement.

General Wadsworth then crossed over with the residue of his brigade, consisting of detachments from Cols. Allen, Bloom's, Stranahan's and Mead's regiments and Col. Fenwick with the light artillery, amounting in all to about 700 men. The command was transferred to Gen. Wadsworth, who commanded in the subsequent operations of the day. After a line had been formed on the heights, our troops were attacked in the rear, by the Indians and Militia, in the direction from Chippawa, and were repulsed and driven back, with great slaughter, and our men remained a second time in quiet possession of the field. At this period General Van Rensselaer ordered over Col. Scott, of the artillery, and Lieut. Totten, the engineers, to lay out a plan of a fortified camp—and immediately after, the General and Maj. Mullany, crossed the river. From the heights, the General observed a strong reinforcement of the enemy from Fort George, marching up under the command of Gen. Sheaffe, who succeeded Gen. Brock in command, amounting to about 6 or 700 men.

As this force, in co-operation with the force of the enemy yet hanging near our flanks, would inevitably overpower our brave troops now fatigued with several hours hard fighting, the General was prevailed to recross the river, in the hope of inducing the militia to cross to the relief of our brave countrymen; not a man of whom could be prevailed upon to cross over. The British militia and Indians, being reinforced by the troops from Fort George, made a vigorous attack, and although opposed by fresh troops, superior in discipline and numbers, yet our men maintained the unequal conflict with a determination, bordering upon desperation, for a considerable time, when all hope of relief being cut off, they capitulated to a superior force, and were conducted prisoners of war to Fort George. Our loss in prisoners and wounded was as follows:

*Wounded.* Of the regulars 62, 2 since dead, 6 dangerous. Of the militia 20, 9 dangerous.

*Prisoners.* Regulars 336, militia 373 besides officers.

There was a brisk exchange of cannon shot during the whole day at the different fortification along the river. The jail & a brewery at Newark, were fired by hot shot from Fort Niagara and consumed.

The corps of General Brock and Col. M'Donald, were conveyed to Newark and interred near the Fort with martial honors. Gen. B. was 55 years of age, a real gentleman, and one of the best generals in the British provinces.

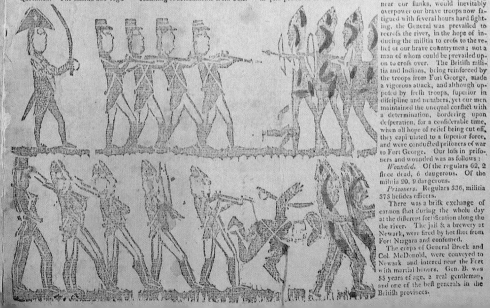

them, governors would not relinquish command of the men to the regular army. New Englanders were the most effective and best equipped of the state military establishments, and their absence contributed to the poor showing of American endeavors in the northeastern theater.

Overall performance was decidedly mixed, in part because of the varied attitudes as well as readiness of different regions. While the best American militia lived in New England, the very place most opposed to the war, the parts of the country most fervent for it—such as Kentucky—often could field only militia more willing than able. When the war went badly, even the willingness began to subside.

Nonetheless, militia could rise to the occasion to fight effectively, as in the Creek War of 1813–1814, and in William Henry Harrison's pursuit of the British and their Indian allies in the fall of 1813, and most famously in the valiant defense of Baltimore and of New Orleans. In addition, militia service was the source of some of the war's most talented generals, men like Harrison, Andrew Jackson, and Jacob Brown, who emerged as resolute and vigorous leaders for whom men would stand and fight. Unfortunately, other chronicles of the militia were not so glowing. They often insisted that they were a defensive force meant to protect homesteads rather than gallivant into foreign countries. Worse, when they did fight, they had a disturbing tendency to run away. The most infamous incident occurred when ragtag units tried to stop the British advance on Washington at Bladensburg. That battle on August 24, 1814, was a devastating humiliation as the militia fled at such a breakneck pace that it was later dubbed the "Bladensburg Races." On the other extreme, frontier militia schooled more in the rigors of the wilderness than the restraint of martial punctilio could match Indian foes blow for vicious blow in committing ugly atrocities.

Even had it not been hampered by lackluster leaders and manpower shortages, American strategy early in the war was at best a muddle. A sensible plan would have been to focus all resources on Montreal, the most populous Canadian town west of impregnable Quebec as well as the region's transportation hub. Taking Montreal would have meant control of all Canada west of it. Yet Americans wasted time and energy on uncoordinated forays, one launched from Detroit, several across the Niagara River, and yet another up Lake Champlain. All of these invasion attempts failed. On the other side, the British and Canadians acted with dispatch and resolve, seizing control of the upper

Great Lakes by taking Fort Mackinac, extending that control south to Detroit and beyond, and defending key points against American assault, such as Queenston.

The British also effectively employed Indian allies in the northern theater of war. In late 1811, Americans had unwittingly helped to forge the Anglo-Indian connection by attacking an extensive intertribal confederation on Tippecanoe Creek where the charismatic Shawnee Tecumseh and his brother Tenskwatawa (known to whites as "the Prophet") had established a headquarters at Prophet's Town. There William Henry Harrison dispersed the Indians and claimed victory, but he had actually driven Tecumseh into the arms of the British.

The repercussions of that partnership for the United States were profound. Tecumseh and his Indian allies augmented sparse Canadian militia and the handful of regulars Britain could spare from the fight with Napoleon. Moreover, the Anglo-Indian alliance sometimes made the northwestern frontier the scene of vicious warfare. The commander at Fort Dearborn negotiated safe passage for his surrendered garrison, but Indians massacred it anyway, including many wives and children. The threat of merciless Indians panicked William Hull into surrendering Detroit in 1812. In early 1813 after a

Westward expansion triggered violence that often escalated and spread racial hatred. The attack on Fort Mims by Red Stick Creeks, retaliation for a militia ambush, prompted Andrew Jackson to vow to "exterminate" the Creeks responsible.

# The Northern Theater

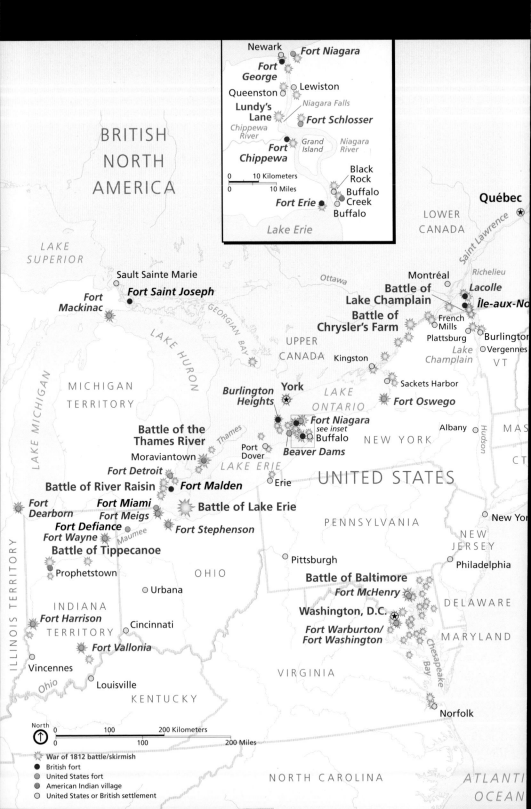

Newark • Fort Niagara
Fort George
Queenston ○ • Lewiston
Niagara Falls
Lundy's Lane
Chippewa River
Fort Chippewa
Grand Island
Niagara River
• Fort Schlosser
Black Rock
Buffalo Creek
Fort Erie •
Buffalo
Lake Erie

0    10 Kilometers
0    10 Miles

BRITISH NORTH AMERICA

LAKE SUPERIOR

Sault Sainte Marie
Fort Saint Joseph
Fort Mackinac

LAKE HURON

GEORGIAN BAY

Ottawa

Québec

LOWER CANADA

Saint Lawrence

Richelieu
Montréal
Battle of Lake Champlain
Lacolle
Île-aux-No[…]
Battle of Chrysler's Farm
French Mills
Plattsburg
Burlington
Lake Champlain
Vergennes
VT

UPPER CANADA
Kingston

MICHIGAN TERRITORY

LAKE MICHIGAN

Burlington Heights
York
LAKE ONTARIO
Sackets Harbor
Fort Oswego

Fort Niagara
see inset
Buffalo
Beaver Dams

Battle of the Thames River
Moraviantown
Thames
Port Dover
LAKE ERIE
Erie

NEW YORK
Albany ○
Hudson
MAS[…]
CT

Fort Detroit
Battle of River Raisin • Fort Malden

UNITED STATES

New Yo[…]

Fort Dearborn
Fort Miami
Fort Meigs
Fort Defiance
Fort Wayne
Maumee
Battle of Lake Erie
• Fort Stephenson

PENNSYLVANIA

NEW JERSEY
Philadelphia

Battle of Tippecanoe
Prophetstown
OHIO
Urbana ○

Pittsburgh ○

Battle of Baltimore
Fort McHenry
Washington, D.C. ★
Fort Warburton/ Fort Washington

DELAWARE

MARYLAND

INDIANA TERRITORY
Fort Harrison
Cincinnati
Fort Vallonia

ILLINOIS TERRITORY

Vincennes ○
Louisville ○
KENTUCKY

VIRGINIA

Chesapeake Bay

Norfolk

North
0    100    200 Kilometers
0    100    200 Miles

Ohio

✳ War of 1812 battle/skirmish
● British fort
● United States fort
● American Indian village
○ United States or British settlement

NORTH CAROLINA

ATLANTIC OCEAN

column commanded by James Winchester was defeated on the River Raisin south of Detroit, Indians slaughtered the American wounded. For the remainder of the war in the Northwest, the cry "Remember the Raisin!" rallied American troops with a grim reminder of this especially brutal aspect of the war.

*The cry "Remember the Raisin!" rallied American troops with a grim reminder of this especially brutal aspect of the war.*

As the Anglo-Indian alliance in Canada indicates, the War of 1812 was in many respects an Indian war, involving American Indians not only in the North but also in the South. A civil war in the powerful Creek confederation of the Mississippi Territory broke out in 1813 pitting Nativists (called Red Sticks) against Creeks who had accommodated, albeit grudgingly, white culture. At first, it had nothing to do with the Anglo-American conflict, but a Red Stick attack on Fort Mims, where a large number of Creeks as well as American settlers had gathered for protection, transformed the struggle into the Creek War, a full-blown contest between the Red Sticks and American territorial and state militias. At the head of Tennessee militia and volunteers, Andrew Jackson became a frontier hero when he all but annihilated the Red Sticks at Tohopeka (Horseshoe Bend) on the Tallapoosa River on March 27, 1814. In one of the war's final chapters, the British tried to enlist the survivors of Horseshoe Bend as allies for their campaign in the Gulf of Mexico, but the battered refugees from the Creek War were of little help.

In fact, Indians who cast their lot with either the British or the Americans eventually had reason to regret it. Jackson fought the Red Sticks with the help of allied Creeks, Cherokees, and Choctaws, only to compel both Indian friends and foes to give up a vast portion of their lands in the Treaty of Fort Jackson. The Anglo-Indian alliance in the North came to pieces when Oliver Hazard Perry's 1813 naval victory on Lake Erie forced British land forces to conduct a rapid withdrawal eastward. William Henry Harrison caught them on the Thames River. Tecumseh was killed in the battle that ensued, which was a major British defeat that reclaimed the Northwest for the Americans while shattering the Indian alliance with the British. It also effectively destroyed Tecumseh's confederation of tribes. Crushed in the South by Jackson and in the North by Harrison, American Indians would be abandoned by their inconstant British friends and were obliged to give up immense areas north of the Ohio as well as east of the Mississippi. It was a prelude to the policy of Indian Removal that Jackson as president would impose on the southern tribes in the 1830s.

The Indian alliance carefully built by Tecumseh crumbled with his death. While neither Americans nor Canadians lost territory at the end of the war, American Indians ceded huge swaths of land along the frontier.

# "Plunder Without Distinction"

As the background of this grand portrait of Sir George Cockburn suggests, his incendiary attack on Washington, DC, ranked as a highlight in his naval career.

Americans living on the Chesapeake Bay paid a steep price for the War of 1812.

For over six months, beginning in the spring of 1813, the British Navy launched amphibious raids on coastal towns and farms, destroying crops, stealing livestock, and encouraging the enslaved to flee. British Rear Admiral George Cockburn disrupted American shipping by blockading the bay.

British attacks on bayside towns, including Norfolk, Virginia, and Frenchtown, Maryland, stirred resentment. "The first step was plunder without distinction," the author of an account of the raid on Havre de Grace claimed. "Wherever the evil genius directed the steps of the enemy . . . conflagration, robbery, waste and devastation were the consequences . . . "

First lady Dolley Madison labeled Cockburn's attacks on civilians as a "savage stile of warfare." Cockburn himself earned the epithet the "Beast of Havre de Grace," and threatened to capture Mrs. Madison and parade her through London's streets. "Fears & alarms" circulated through the capital city. Newspapers printed sensational tales of British atrocities and rumors circulated of attacks on women.

Following a winter respite, the war returned to the Chesapeake with renewed fury. Governor General George Prevost decided to avenge American attacks in Canada and weaken the United States in other theaters of the war by forcing troops to regroup to defend their capital.

The British landed in Maryland in mid-August 1814, burned Washington, captured Alexandria, and bombarded Fort McHenry. The attacks were bad enough, but the Corps of Colonial Marines, recruited from enslaved blacks, marched with the British sowing seeds of racial paranoia.

Civilians were not insulated from the ravages of the war. Along the Niagara River and Lake Ontario, raids became rapacious and retaliatory. The British claimed it all began in April 1813 when Brigadier General Zebulon Montgomery Pike led a naval-borne force across Lake Ontario to attack Upper Canada's capital of York (modern Toronto). Pike prohibited wanton destruction and looting, but debris from an exploded powder magazine killed him, and his enraged men turned their anger on the town. What they could not pilfer they burned. Worse was to come. When Americans abandoned Fort George at the mouth of the Niagara in December 1813, they burned the nearby village of Newark. It was a remarkably cruel deed, leaving the town's civilians without shelter in the dead of winter and forcing them in bitter cold to trek through the deep snow to distant towns. General Sir Gordon Drummond soon avenged Newark with an attack on Fort Niagara in which British soldiers bayoneted Americans as they were surrendering.

The British rampaged all along the Niagara, burning Buffalo, Lewiston, and Black Rock, and provoking retaliation in kind from Americans into the spring of 1814. The result was a desolate landscape of burned-out farms and deserted villages. Citing these incidents, the British justified pitiless war elsewhere. Their raiding tactics in Chesapeake Bay in 1813 and 1814 and the torching of Washington's public buildings in August 1814, including the Capitol and Executive Mansion, were supposed to even the score for York and Newark. But the raid on the capital was of little strategic importance, and world opinion frowned on what seemed an act of petulant vandalism.

The year 1814 decided the war, but with unexpected results. Americans abandoned any thoughts of offensive operations and braced for a wave of British invasions. In Europe, the distraction of Napoleon came to an end in mid-1814 when he was defeated and forced into exile, requiring the United States to face the prospect of thousands of seasoned British veterans becoming available for the war in North America. The British planned accordingly. In the summer of 1814, Sir George Prevost moved by land and water out of Canada along the traditional New York invasion route of Lake Champlain. In addition to taking the fight to the United States, the campaign intended to isolate disaffected New England states and possibly persuade them to make a separate peace. The raids in Chesapeake Bay were to prevent American troops from moving north to resist the British advance and to target the home ports

Though of limited strategic importance, the British attack on Washington, DC, dealt a chilling blow to American morale. It's hard to imagine what went through William Strickland's mind when he created this etching of the scorched Capitol (above). William Thornton's watercolor depicts how the burning of the capital was seared into national memory.

BRITISH NORTH
AMERICA

UPPER
CANADA

*Richelieu*

Montréal

**Battle of
Lake Champlain**

VERMONT

Burlington

*Lake
Champlain*

Vergennes

*Kennebec*

**Fort Sullivan**
Eastport
Machias
**Fort
O'Brie**
Hampden
Castine
Belfast

Portland

LAKE
ONTARIO

**Fort Oswego**

NEW YORK

Albany

*Hudson*

NEW
HAMPSHIRE

Portsmouth

Marblehead
Charlestown
Provincetown

UNITED STATES

MASSACHUSETTS

Worcester

**Boston**

Hartford

CONNECTICUT

R. I.

Newport

New London

New York

*Martha's
Vineyard*

*Nantucket*

*Cape
Cod*

*Long Island Sound*

*Block
Island*

*British Blockade of United States Ports*

ATLANTIC
OCEAN

PENNSYLVANIA

*Susquehanna*

*Delaware*

Trenton

Philadelphia

NEW
JERSEY

*Delaware
Bay*

**Battle of Baltimore**
**Fort McHenry**

MARYLAND

**Washington, D.C.**
**Fort Warburton/
Fort Washington**

*see inset*

DELAWARE

*Chesapeake Bay*

Richmond

VIRGINIA

Hampton

Norfolk

**North**

MARYLAND

Frederick

*Potomac*

Havre de Grace

Principio

Frenchtown

Baltimore

**Fort McHenry**

North
Point

Fredericktown

Georgetown

Georgetown

Annapolis

**Washington D.C.**
Alexandria
**Fort Washington**

Bladensburg

Upper
Marlboro

*Chesapeake Bay*

DEL.

VIRGINIA

Benedict

0      20 Kilometers
0      20 Miles

North

0        100        200 Kilometers
0        100        200 Miles

✳ War of 1812 battle/skirmish
● United States fort
○ United States or British settlement

After the assault on Washington, the combined British force moved on Baltimore.

And then miraculously for the Americans everything fell apart for the British. On paper Prevost's New York invasion looked irresistible and promised a quick path to final victory, but the enterprise rapidly unraveled when the British lost a key battle on both land and water at Plattsburgh on September 11, 1814. Without naval forces to keep his supply lines intact, Prevost could not continue southward. He headed back to Canada. Similarly the British assault on Baltimore failed when stubborn American militia, including some units that had taken flight at Bladensburg, stood their ground and the bastion of Fort McHenry withstood the Royal Navy's relentless bombardment, denying passage to the city's Inner Harbor. By mid-September 1814, the vaunted British offensives in the northern and eastern theaters had ended in failure despite their enormous advantages of greater numbers, more experienced soldiers, and a seemingly irresistible momentum in defeating Napoleon. Everyone was surprised.

Yet the greatest surprise of the war was yet to take place. A third British strike of 1814 was aimed at New Orleans on America's soft underbelly, the coast of the Gulf of Mexico. British success in the gulf would have imperiled the entire Mississippi Valley, and possibly would have altered the outcome of the war, regardless of the battle there occurring after the conclusion of peace negotiations. At New Orleans, Andrew Jackson commanded an ungainly assortment of 7,000 men, including sailors, regulars, buccaneers, and Frenchmen, along with militia from Louisiana, Kentucky, and Tennessee, some of them lacking weapons. Two Louisiana regiments of about 400 free black volunteers were part of the defense as well.

Andrew Jackson emerged as a celebrated hero of the war. Alexis de Tocqueville wrote that Jackson became president "solely by the recollection of a victory which he gained, twenty years ago, under the walls of New Orleans."

The British, accustomed to militia running like frightened rabbits, derisively called the Americans defending New Orleans "dirty shirts." Six months earlier, American and British forces had slugged out a bloody stalemate at Lundy's Lane near Niagara Falls, a battle so costly that all four main commanders under both Stars and Stripes and Union Jack were wounded. But the grudging respect won at Lundy's Lane was blithely cast aside by the swaggering British outside of New Orleans. After all, the redcoats reasoned, they had some 8,000 seasoned veterans, control of the Mississippi and Lake Borgne, and no less than the Duke of Wellington's brother-in-law, Lieutenant General

Sir Edward Pakenham, at their head. But the Americans did not run, and the British frontal assault on January 8, 1815, dealt them the most crushing defeat of the entire war. More than 2,000 were killed or wounded in half an hour. American casualties numbered fewer than a hundred.

The news about New Orleans reached the capital in early February 1815, shortly before the treaty of peace arrived from Europe, linking the two events in the public mind as proof that the British defeat on the gulf meant the United States had won the war. This was hardly the case, of course. American land campaigns in the War of 1812 were almost all failures. With the exception of Harrison on the Thames River, every assault on Canada miscarried, and except for stalwart behavior at such places as Chippewa, Plattsburgh, Baltimore, and New Orleans, militia and regulars alike rarely covered themselves with glory. A major consequence of the war on land, however, was a discernment that militia alone was insufficient for national defense. After the war, concerted efforts to promote professionalism in the officer corps led to innovations and improvements in the curriculum and organization of the United States Military Academy. And for a time, Americans maintained a larger standing army than had been politically possible before the war. Yet enthusiasm for that policy gradually faded as years passed uneventfully and the country looked westward, the war itself to become, in the words of one historian, "America's forgotten conflict."

*Jeanne T. Heidler is professor of history at the US Air Force Academy, where she is the senior civilian in her department. David is an independent scholar. Their most recent book is* Henry Clay: The Essential American (*New York: Random House, 2010*).

> *But the Americans did not run, and the British frontal assault on January 8, 1815, dealt them the most crushing defeat of the entire war.*

When combined land and naval forces turned back a British invasion at Plattsburgh, New York, they denied British peace negotiators any territorial claims based on enemy land captured during the war.

# Fighting for Freedom: African Americans and the War of 1812

By Gene Allen Smith

*In June 1807, the United States and Great Britain appeared on the verge of conflict: After the frigate* Leopard *fired on the US warship* Chesapeake, *British sailors boarded the American vessel, mustered the crew, and impressed four seamen—Jenkins Ratford, William Ware, Daniel Martin, and John Strachan—whom they claimed were deserters. The damaged* Chesapeake *limped back to Norfolk with three dead and eighteen wounded.*

The *Chesapeake-Leopard* affair represented one of the most demeaning episodes in the early history of the United States. Associated with events that caused the second Anglo-American war, this affair involved the act of boarding a neutral ship and forcing sailors to serve aboard British warships, both thorny diplomatic issues that divided the two countries well into the 19th century. Even more significant, three of the four impressed sailors—Martin, Strachan, and Ware—were black men and all claimed to be Americans who had been impressed. During the debates and protests that followed, race did not figure into the national dialogue. Nonetheless it remained central in this episode and in the history of the War of 1812.

As during the American Revolution, black sailors and soldiers saw the second war with Britain as a means to advance their own agenda. For free blacks, the War of 1812 provided the chance to broker their participation in ways that enhanced their individual and collective status within society. Yet for free blacks, the war did not advance their march toward equality but rather initiated a new era of prejudice and racial discrimination. For enslaved peoples, serving as participants could provide an avenue to freedom, but it did not happen as often as expected.

**A battalion of free blacks, many refugees from Santo Domingo, fighting alongside Choctaw Indians, helped slow the British advance on New Orleans.**

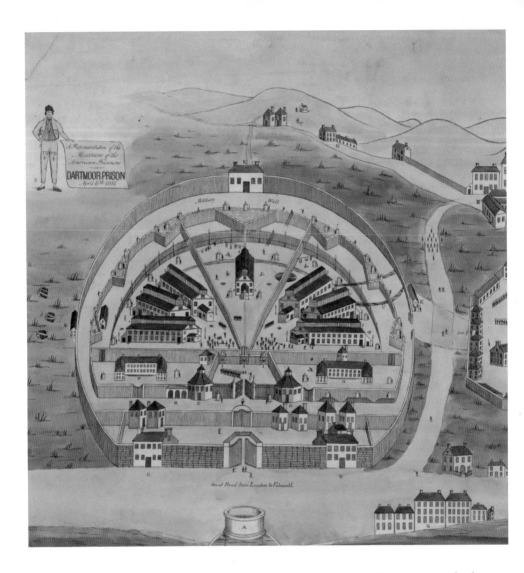

Great Britain held American prisoners of war, including perhaps 1,000 African American seamen, in Dartmoor Prison. Still confined months after the Treaty of Ghent, the prisoners rioted. Guards killed seven and wounded about sixty in the "Dartmoor Massacre" of 1815.

After the Revolutionary War the US government had chosen to limit the size of the American army, and this ultimately created opportunities for free blacks and slaves. The traditional fears of a large standing army, as well as burdening fiscal concerns, carried great considerations and prompted Americans to rely upon citizen soldiers. The 1792 federal militia act further defined the role of American citizens in defending their country by placing responsibility for arming the militia on the individual and making states responsible for training and enforcement of the federal and state statutes. Each state did have the authority to clarify the federal mandate, even though most simply mimicked the wording of the 1792 act. New Jersey (1792), Vermont (1797), North Carolina (1806), and New Hampshire (1808) required free white male citizens to serve but took no position on African Americans. Some states such as North Carolina and Virginia permitted blacks to muster alongside whites. Others such as Connecticut (1784), Massachusetts (1785), and South Carolina (1800) exempted blacks from the militia altogether; South Carolina even forbade "negroes" to be "armed with any offensive weapons unless in cases of alarm." The action of the states did not create any significant problems for the country as there were no serious "alarms" or crises necessitating troops. But by the early 19th century America's difficulties with Britain and with various American Indian tribes on the northwestern frontier forced a reevaluation of the federal mandate.

Prior to 1807 Detroit, Michigan, slave Peter Denison had been indentured to Elijah Brush for a year, after which Brush granted Denison his freedom. Apparently Brush had taken this action without the knowledge or approval of his owner, Catherine Tucker. Tucker protested the emancipation and demanded Denison's return, and a subsequent writ of habeas corpus on behalf of Denison forced the Michigan territorial government to decide on the slavery question. Judge Augustus Woodward ruled in the case that Denison remained Catherine Tucker's property, that property rights would be upheld, and that any bondsman living in the territory as of May 31, 1793, and belonging to a slaveholder as of July 11, 1796—the day Britain turned the territory over to the United States—would remain a slave. Although the Northwest Ordinance had forbidden slavery in the territory after 1787, the lands the British turned over to the United States in 1796 fell under a different interpretation and Denison technically remained a slave.

This story may be similar to that of other early 19th-century slaves who tried through the courts to secure their freedom, but Denison's tale differed. After the 1807 *Chesapeake-Leopard* affair territorial governor William Hull offered Denison "a written license," permitting him to form a militia company of free blacks and runaway slaves. Apparently Denison had gained the confidence of Detroit's black population, and according to Hull, under his leadership segregated troops "frequently appeared under arms" and "made considerable progress in military discipline." Hull maintained that these men demonstrated an unquestioned "attachment to our government, and a determination to aid in the defense of the country." The crisis that prompted Hull to turn to Denison and the city's black population soon passed and the governor disbanded the militia.

*The traditional fears of a large standing army... prompted Americans to rely upon citizen soldiers.*

Many of Denison's men had fled from bondage in Canada to the freedom of Michigan; this short-lived southern exodus undermines the traditional image of the underground railroad leading north to Canada and freedom. During the late 1700s and early 1800s the route to freedom most commonly led enslaved peoples south from British Canada to free American territories in the Old Northwest. Canada had phased out slavery in 1793, but not all enslaved people had gained immediate freedom; the institution ended over time, which meant that the Michigan Territory held out the prospect of immediate freedom to those brave enough to cross the treacherous waters of the Detroit River. Yet by the end of the War of 1812, few enslaved people lived in Canada and Canadian law prohibited the further introduction of slavery. This reality prompted enslaved Americans to venture along a well-trodden path or "underground railroad," yet thereafter north to a new Canadian land of freedom.

During the summer of 1812 Governor Hull issued commissions to Captain Denison, to Lieutenant Ezra Burgess, and to Ensign Bossett—all three black men. Hull insisted that the segregated militia of free blacks and runaways were free citizens of the Michigan Territory, and they, like white citizens, could bear arms in times of crisis. They would shortly be needed as the United States declared war on Britain during June 1812, and Detroit would be the first theater of operations; Denison was apparently captured when Hull surrendered the city to British General Isaac Brock.

By 1816 a black Peter Dennison reportedly lived as a free man in the community of Sandwich and attended the St. John's Church of England, just east across the river from Detroit. Perhaps this Denison, now listed as Dennison, spelled his name differently or did not correct the church secretary. In either case, he, his wife, and his other children most likely crossed over into Canada, illustrating how within a few short years the path to freedom had shifted dramatically north to the freedom of Canada. Peter Denison undoubtedly seized this opportunity to relocate north to Canada, purportedly as a free man.

Though the United States did not officially declare war on Spain, its southern neighbor, during this era of conflict border problems along the Gulf of Mexico frontier exacerbated tensions and prompted the Patriot War of 1812–13. During this regional conflict, American settlers living in Florida organized an uprising against Spanish

*Britain's campaign in the mid-Atlantic states created a serious problem for American planters: It emboldened slaves to flight while also making the countryside virtually indefensible.*

rule and coaxed US forces to intervene on their behalf. These Florida Patriots, fearing the chaos in Spain would leave the peninsula vulnerable to foreign occupation, launched a campaign against St. Augustine and the city's black troops. Enslaved peoples had fled to Florida from the American colonies since the late 17th century and the Spanish government and military had warmly received them as a means of bolstering isolated segments of their far-flung empire. St. Augustine had mustered an all-black militia unit as early as 1683, and seven years later King Charles II issued a royal proclamation freeing all slaves who fled to Florida and accepted conversion and baptism. This proclamation created an atmosphere of acceptance for blacks and mulattoes, and permitted the Spanish to incorporate them into the community by instilling ideas of civic pride and military obligations. Most of these numerous runaways fought against the American Patriots in the attempt to protect their tenuous freedom.

Prince Witten, apparently born about 1756 in South Carolina, had escaped from Georgia to Spanish St. Augustine with his family around 1786, after several previously failed attempts. The skilled carpenter registered in

**As this complex political cartoon shows, British attempts to undermine the American slave economy raised both contempt and fear. Here, John Bull—the embodiment of Great Britain—and a British soldier tempt two grotesquely caricatured black men to abandon the tools of agricultural labor and take up arms against the edifice of democracy, preying upon American racial prejudices.**

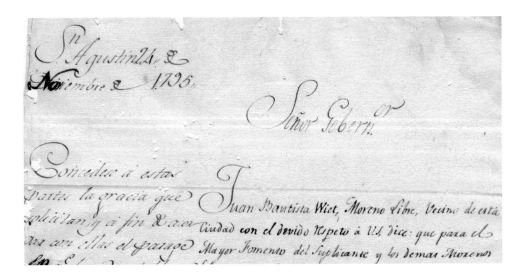

Prince Witten, a fugitive from slavery in Georgia, successfully petitioned for citizenship and freedom in Florida under Spanish law. During the war, Witten fought with the Seminole against the Americans.

1798 with Florida Governor Vincent Manuel de Zéspedes as required, and soon hired himself out as a carpenter in the area. By 1801 Witten had become a captain of the Florida black militia when his son-in-law Jorge Jacobo assumed command of the unit. Thereafter Witten distinguished himself, winning accolades from his Spanish rulers and disdain and contempt from his American enemies. Witten commanded the local black militia when they won the most important engagement of the Patriot War in September 1812, and by doing so, he achieved the distinction of becoming a black officer. But unfortunately, Witten's local accolades could not alter the changing geopolitics of the Gulf Coast of the postwar period when Americans swept across the region and acquired Florida: Witten and his family, along with most of the other St. Augustine blacks, evacuated to Cuba when the Spanish departed in 1821.

When the War of 1812 came in full force to the Chesapeake Bay region, it created new opportunities for slaves who wanted to flee with the British to freedom. During April 1814 Admiral Alexander F.I. Cochrane issued a bold proclamation freeing enslaved people who joined the British cause; this was similar to Lord Dunmore's attempt to mobilize Virginia blacks during the American Revolution. The active presence of British forces in the Chesapeake and along the South Atlantic Coast created opportunities for several thousand enslaved peoples to flee to freedom. Additionally, some 600 former slaves donned uniforms as Colonial Marines and participated in British operations against Washington, Baltimore, and along the South Atlantic. Britain's campaign in the mid-Atlantic states created a serious problem for American planters: It emboldened slaves to flight while also making the countryside virtually indefensible. Should the American militia be called out to confront a British threat, then slaves had free reign to flee or rise against their masters. British forces exploited that fear, leaving Americans in the region doubly exposed—threatened by a potential British invasion if the militia remained in the neighborhoods or exposed to a potential slave revolt if the militia advanced to meet the British threat. This dichotomy provided slaves with unusual opportunities.

Like many enslaved people, Charles Ball used the uncertainties of the era to declare himself free. Born into slavery around 1780, Ball lived on a Calvert County, Maryland, tobacco farm until the owner's death forced the liquidation of the estate. About 1800, Ball's elderly master hired the then 20-year-old slave out at the Washington Navy Yard, with Ball becoming a cook aboard the US frigate *Congress*. Ball fondly remembered his time aboard the ship because officers and sailors treated him well, giving him clothing and money. During this time he also met a host of black sailors who told him stories of freedom in the north and equality at sea. In May 1813, Ball joined a party of white Americans who visited the British fleet in the Chesapeake. He tried unsuccessfully to convince fleeing slaves to return to their masters. Although Ball could have joined with the British and assured his freedom by being evacuated from America, he instead falsely claimed that he was free. When British operations intensified during the spring of 1814, Ball enlisted in Joshua Barney's Chesapeake flotilla, serving aboard a gunboat until the Americans scuttled them. He then served in the artillery alongside Barney's flotillamen at Bladensburg and later helped man the defenses at Baltimore. Once the war ended, Ball remained in Baltimore, and through his economy and hard work, by 1830 he had accumulated money and property. Yet Ball's dream would soon end, as he would be re-enslaved.

Seven years after being sold to a Georgia trader, Charles Ball made his way back to Maryland shortly before war broke out in the Chesapeake. Many years later, Ball recollected standing his ground at the Battle of Bladensburg "until the Commodore [Joshua Barney] was shot down."

Ned Simmons lived most of his life enslaved on Dungeness plantation, on the estate of General Nathanael Greene on Georgia's Cumberland Island. Born in 1763, probably in South Carolina, Simmons' legal status rotated among the Greene family, but his monotonous existence on the island changed very little until the waning weeks of the War of 1812. When Admiral George Cockburn's ships and soldiers invaded the area during early 1815, Simmons immediately volunteered for British military service. He received an old 1808 version of a British red uniform, a weapon,

The Tabby House, named for the mix of oyster shells, lime, and sand used in construction, dates to the tenure of the Nathanael Greene family on Cumberland Island.

and began training to be a Colonial Marine. Then disaster struck! Although Simmons had enlisted, his training had not yet taken him off of Cumberland Island. During early March 1815, two American commissioners arrived to inform the British of the ratification of the peace agreement, and after days of bickering between the commissioners and Cockburn about property, the admiral acquiesced: only property—including slaves—on Cumberland Island at 11 pm on February 17, 1815, would be returned. Even this narrow interpretation of the Treaty of Ghent adversely affected Simmons. He had been one of the first to volunteer, but he had not yet departed the island. On March 10, 1815, British officers stripped Simmons of his uniform, insignia, and his weapon, and he and eighty other men returned to slavery on Cumberland Island. Unfortunately Simmons remained enslaved on Cumberland Island until Federal troops liberated him in 1863, almost fifty years after his first flirtation with freedom.

Born into slavery in Georgia on October 14, 1800, to African and European parents, Jordan Noble had arrived in New Orleans sometime in 1812. The teenage Noble joined the US Army in 1813 as a free drummer in the Seventh US Regiment, and during the fierce night fighting of December 23, 1814, he kept a steady beat as Jackson's troops surprised a British vanguard, delaying the enemy's assault south of the city. By late December two battalions of "Free Men of Color" as well as other free black militiamen and slave volunteers had swollen Jackson's defenses at nearby Chalmette by more than 900 men. The general's heterogeneous force—consisting of US Army soldiers, free blacks, slaves, Louisiana Creoles, Tennessee and Kentucky frontiersmen, Jean Lafitte's Baratarian privateers, and a small contingent of Choctaw Indians—entrenched behind a defensive rampart on the east side of the Mississippi River, some seven miles south of New Orleans, to meet a series of British attacks during late December 1814 and early January 1815. On January 8, 1815, "the rattle of [Noble's] drum was heard [even] amidst the din of battle," "in the hottest hell of fire" during the unsuccessful chaotic main British frontal assault at Chalmette. After the battle the British evacuated from the Gulf Coast while Noble and his free black compatriots remained in New Orleans. In fact, Jordan Noble maintained his military connections and participated in the 1836 Seminole War in Florida, in the Mexican War, and with Confederate and Union forces during the Civil War; Noble claimed service during four American wars. After his fighting days had passed, Noble held tightly onto his position within the New Orleans free black community and onto his military legacy as the

*The rattle of [Noble's] drum was heard [even] amidst the din of battle...*

Jordan Noble also served as a drummer in the Mexican War and rallied free men of color to defend New Orleans from Federal attack during the Civil War, when he used this ca. 1860 drum.

Ethel Magafan's mural, painted during the Great Depression for the Recorder of Deeds Building in Washington, DC, portrays the diversity of Jackson's army in the defense of New Orleans.

drummer boy of the Battle of New Orleans. His distinction and talent, combined with his intense patriotism, had also permitted Noble to navigate the perils associated with pre– and post–Civil War American race relations.

The documentary record that chronicles black service during the War of 1812 is very fragmentary at best. Peter Denison, Prince Witten, Charles Ball, Ned Simmons, and Jordan Noble all chose sides during the War of 1812, and these choices ultimately defined their individual and collective identities. As their stories testify, men of African descent did serve as soldiers and sailors aboard warships and on privateers during the war in substantial numbers on either side; nearly 1,000 African American sailors were captured and held in Britain's notorious Dartmoor Prison—and they embraced their status as free black seamen struggling to uphold their belief in "Free Trade and Sailors' Rights." Some 600 Chesapeake Bay slaves joined the British Colonial Marines and marched with redcoats

on Washington, DC, and Baltimore, while others chose to remain with their masters and fight for the Americans. The American army had not opened its enlistments to black troops, and most states did not permit blacks to muster. There were no all-black regular army units in 1812 and 1813, and the black presence, when noted, was poorly documented. Along the coast of Georgia and South Carolina enslaved peoples faced the same choices as did those in the Chesapeake, while along the Gulf Coast they found additional choices—some joined with the Spanish, with Native American tribes, and others with Andrew Jackson or the British. Jackson ultimately secured the assistance of most with promises of freedom and equality that never fully appeared.

In some instances, the feats of men like Denison were recorded for posterity, but the stories of noncombatants are chronicled often only in statistics. In the Chesapeake, as many as 4,000 to 5,000 enslaved people fled to British

> *[Free blacks']
> patriotic efforts had
> not reshaped white
> minds about what
> role they should play
> in society, and public
> memories of the war
> largely ignored their
> contributions.*

protection and were evacuated to Bermuda, Canada, or Trinidad. In New York, Philadelphia, and Baltimore, enslaved people and free blacks worked alongside whites to dig entrenchments for those cities, loudly proclaiming their civic and patriotic duty. Yet, black-white relations worsened after the war. Collectively, black unity had demonstrated a powerful threat, engendering fears in white America that were exacerbated by memories of the recent revolution in nearby Haiti (1791–1804). In the aftermath of the conflict, Americans destroyed free mulatto gulf communities in former Spanish Florida that they viewed as a threat to peace and as a challenge to the white *status quo*. Later, the removal of American Indians east of the Mississippi River bolstered the southern plantation system, creating the Cotton Kingdom of the mid-1800s and further altering race relations. Meanwhile, in British dominions, former American enslaved people clutched tenaciously to the freedom they obtained with evacuation, though the British government abandoned them in a segregated naval base in Bermuda or herded them into ill-provisioned camps in Canada and then into unsettled regions of Trinidad; they struggled economically, but they remained free.

In the end, the War of 1812 did not provide greater opportunities or equality for free blacks as they anticipated, nor did it initiate a wave of emancipation for enslaved Americans seeking freedom. They would find themselves wedged between slavery and freedom, and between race discrimination and egalitarianism. Their patriotic efforts had not reshaped white minds about what role they should play in society, and public memories of the war largely ignored their contributions. New prejudicial racial distinctions replaced class differences among blacks and destroyed once and for all the optimism of the Revolutionary era. For African Americans, the "forgotten war" delayed their quest for equality and freedom.

*Gene Allen Smith is professor of history at Texas Christian University in Fort Worth, Texas. He is author or editor of several books, including an edited reprint of Arsène Lacarrière Latour's* Historical Memoir of the War in West Florida and Louisiana in 1814–15 *(Gainesville: University Press of Florida, 1999),* Thomas ap Catesby Jones: Commodore of Manifest Destiny *(Annapolis, MD: Naval Institute Press, 2000), and* The Slaves' Gamble: Choosing Sides in the War of 1812 *(New York, Palgrave Macmillan, 2013).*

**Jordan Noble was among the 90 free veterans of color who finally were permitted to march in New Orleans' "Glorious Eighth" parade in 1851, achieving community recognition and honor long overdue.**

A colored veteran of
1814-15, who beat the drum
for Major D'Aquin's
Battalion. —

E. C. Wharton
Apl 20/67

# Legacies: The War of 1812 in American Memory

By Matthew Dennis

*If the War of 1812 played a more important role in American public memory, it would likely have earned a less generic name. The war is the only one in American history designated simply by the year of its commencement, and for nearly a hundred years after it ended in 1815, its name hardly even qualified as a proper noun.*

As its centennial approached in 1915, it often appeared in print in merely descriptive terms, typically with a lower-case "w"—"the war of 1812"—lacking some other, grander or more definitive label. A children's book published in 1884, *History of the United States in Words of One Syllable*, devoted two pages to the struggle and concluded, "This was known for a time as the 'Late War,' but since then we have had more wars, so it would not do to call it by that name now." Yet the author, Helen W. Pierson, offered America's children nothing in its place before moving on with her glorious tale. The claim forwarded by some, that the war was America's Second War of Independence, had not caught on in the 1880s, nor has it since. As a recent historian of the war, Alan Taylor, has written, "the War of 1812 looms small in American memory."

What should we make of the war's low profile in American public memory? The accomplishments of the War of 1812 were meager, and general historical knowledge of it is thin compared to the transformational struggles that bookended it—the American Revolution and the Civil War. And the war's legacy in popular memory and imagination is thinner still—not well informed historically, more mythic, and strikingly ephemeral. So, we might ask: How has the war been remembered? How has it affected American legend and lore? And, more intriguingly: Why has it been so readily forgotten?

After Eben Appleton donated the Star-Spangled Banner to the Smithsonian Institution during the war's centennial, the aging national icon—like the memory of the war itself—underwent a series of restorations.

If the War of 1812 was largely a series of military disasters for the United States, the Treaty of Ghent that ended it was a windfall and godsend. Signed in Belgium on Christmas Eve in 1814, copies arrived in Washington on February 14, 1815. The Senate ratified the pact two days later. Though the treaty did not actually address the primary issues that propelled the country to war, by 1815 Americans were generally happy to accept a stalemate with the British. The political objectives of President James Madison and the Democratic-Republicans determined how the war would be characterized publically in its immediate aftermath—as a glorious victory, a heroic defense of the United States.

General Andrew Jackson's victory in the Battle of New Orleans on January 8, 1815, though tardy, proved timely. It was real enough and recent enough that it could help obscure the memory of the military debacles that began with General William Hull's disgraceful defeat and surrender at Detroit in August of 1812. Similarly, American maritime triumphs and the war's genuine naval heroes were immediately marketable. Troubling details like the ill-famed Dartmoor incident could contradict the popular party line, but the American public—as much as Madison—seemed relatively uninterested in less auspicious facts.

When the release of American prisoners held at Dartmoor in England was delayed in the spring of 1815, some detainees grew restless. On April 6, guards overreacted to their agitation and shot into a crowd, killing seven and wounding about sixty. American accounts quickly represented the tragedy as "the Dartmoor Massacre," threatening the new peace and dampening the buoyant tone of the American postwar narrative. A joint American-British investigation judged the incident to be an unfortunate accident, and the British provided compensation. The Madison administration was able to calm tensions and derail a storyline that Americans sought to avoid—one that cast them as victims rather than heroes. Survivors would later publish their own potentially inflammatory accounts in the United States, but these, along with pension petitions that offered non-heroic personal tales of loss and pain, could not compete with the celebratory patriotic narrative that dominated the public sphere.

If American public memory rejected victimhood in the wake of the Dartmoor Massacre, it seemed to embrace it conditionally and purposefully earlier, following the infamous River Raisin Massacre of January 1813. General James Winchester had moved his small army of Kentucky

*Political objectives... determined how the war would be characterized publically after its immediate aftermath—as a glorious victory, a historic defense of the United States.*

This classical allegory for the Treaty of Ghent ignored the near disasters of the war. Instead, in this fantasy, Minerva—the embodiment of war—dictates peace terms to a humbled Britannia as the triumphant Columbia rides toward victory.

volunteers imprudently north from the Maumee Valley in Ohio toward Frenchtown, along the River Raisin south of British-held Detroit, to rescue its inhabitants. Momentarily successful, the Americans rashly advanced too close to the enemy and too far from any possible support. A few days later, Winchester's men were overpowered by a superior force of British regulars, militia, and Indians; what began as a credible defense degenerated into panic, defeat, deaths, and surrender. On January 23, Indian allies of the British massacred some 30 to 60 wounded American prisoners left behind in Frenchtown. The incident shocked and embarrassed the British. It enflamed the Americans. The cry "Remember the Raisin" was seared into American public consciousness. Plundering, scalping, and atrocities besmirched the records of both sides in the conflict, but the horrific events at the River Raisin enabled an American propaganda war that charged the British with treachery, advanced the Democratic-Republicans' war agenda, and diverted attention from the ineptitude of its military efforts. Celebration of these victims aided recruitment; more importantly, it renewed familiar charges of Native savagery and sparked new eruptions of Indian-hating, even though Native people served on both sides in the war.

If Americans ultimately failed in their effort to conquer Canada, the war significantly advanced their conquest of

*"Victory" in the War of 1812 unleashed a wave of American patriotism after 1815, which ironically emphasized the triumph of the American Revolution more than the split decision of the "Late War."*

the West against Native peoples struggling to preserve their homelands. At the Battle of the Thames in 1813, US forces prevailed and killed Tecumseh, a Native leader critical to pan-tribal resistance. Along the country's southwestern frontiers, General Andrew Jackson defeated the divided Creeks, which would effectively open up millions of acres for the westward expansion of the Cotton South. The Treaty of Ghent ending the war stipulated that the United States guarantee to western Indians the same status and territory as they possessed in 1811. But the *status quo ante bellum* (the state that existed before the war) was not really restored. US negotiators signed 14 treaties between July and October 1815 but returned no land. Forget? Though the British government showed some concern for their Native allies—allies who had contributed significantly to their defense of Canada—they ultimately abandoned them to their unpromising fate, as they faced new waves of expansion by the American republic. White Americans soon forgot how tenuous their "victory" in the West had been, and few beyond the Old Northwest continued to remember the Raisin.

"Victory" in the War of 1812 unleashed a wave of American patriotism after 1815, which ironically emphasized the triumph of the American Revolution more than the split decision of the "Late War." The glories of the latter struggle—such as they were—were rendered indistinct as the war was subsumed by Revolutionary memory. 1812–1815 seemed to ratify the popular memory of 1776 and 1783, igniting a new nationalism, expressed in politics, festive commemorations, architecture, arts, and literature.

Infamously, the British had sacked Washington, DC, in August 1814 and destroyed nearly all its public buildings, including the Capitol and President's Mansion. Famously, Dolley Madison had managed to save Gilbert Stuart's full-length portrait of George Washington, which seems fitting, as Washington would remain the nation's greatest hero. Though the ruined interior would require major renovation, the smoke-stained exterior of the president's house soon received a bright coat of paint. The Capitol too was restored, and plans laid for a new Rotunda. In 1817, the renowned history painter John Trumbull won a commission for four life-size pictures to adorn it, all focusing on achievements of the Revolution. These paintings, completed between 1817 and 1824 and reproduced as engravings, won a broad, appreciative audience; they were ultimately installed in the Capitol in 1826, the nation's jubilee.

Although some dubbed the War of 1812 "Mr. Madison's War," it was Mrs. Madison—Dolley Madison—who burnished her reputation with wartime grit.

Even 200 years later, history books retell how Mrs. Madison saved George Washington's portrait. As British invaders approached, Dolley directed White House staff—including President Madison's enslaved manservant, Paul Jennings—to break the portrait's frame, remove the canvas, and rescue it from capture or incineration.

Mrs. Madison's fame, however, rested on a lifetime of accomplishment not one event. Born into a Quaker family, Dolley met James Madison in Philadelphia after the death of her first husband, John Todd. She occasionally served as widower Thomas Jefferson's White House hostess. But her real contribution can be traced to her own tenure as "presidentess."

Biographer Catherine Allgor argues that Dolley's social activities and her ability to build bipartisan bridges "legitimized her husband's administration to the nation and the world and went a long way to establishing Washington City as a capital." She masterfully used "conciliation to disarm and defuse a violent political culture."

Only after Mrs. Madison brought her blend of intelligence and charm to the White House did an enduring role for the president's spouse emerge. Her parties delighted guests with surprises, perhaps embellished, like a "magnificent pink dome of ice cream." Her open houses added a sparkle of the ceremonial to the democratic, and a dose of the resolute in time of crisis.

Thankfully, President Zachary Taylor takes credit for retiring the title "presidentess" by using the term "first lady" for the first time at Dolley Madison's 1849 funeral.

**Twentieth-century advertising coopted and further embellished Dolley Madison's reputation as the hostess who served ice cream in the White House.**

of the Revolutionary War. Given its unimpressive history and divisiveness, it made sense to wrap the late war in the sacred, unifying public memory of the Revolution, as President James Monroe did at a massive commemoration at Bunker Hill on July 4, 1817. There he appealed to shared patriotic recollections in the region most estranged during the War of 1812. In Charlestown, the Bunker Hill martyr Joseph Warren proved to be a more plausible and useful hero than, say, the local non-hero General Henry Dearborn, who had ineffectively commanded American forces on the Canadian frontier from 1812 to 1813.

American public memory was transformed in these years in two significant ways—it was diversified and democratized to include common soldiers and sailors and to emphasize heroic maritime achievements largely absent during the Revolution. Necessity was the mother of invention, as naval heroes were abundant in the 1812–1815 conflict— Isaac Hull, Stephen Decatur, William Bainbridge, James Lawrence, Thomas Macdonough, Oliver Hazard Perry— while military champions (Jackson excepted) were not. The army's limited successes were attributed to the heroic endurance of regular soldiers and volunteers, occurring despite—not because of—their military leaders.

Informal gatherings of veterans, organized locally, took place throughout the 1800s and kept memories alive. In New York City, for example, a group of ex-officers and soldiers formed a

Aging veterans, like these gray-bearded "Old Defenders" at the annual remembrance of the Battle of Baltimore (ca.1876–80), have played a consistent role in the commemoration of the war.

mixed Revolutionary War/War of 1812 veterans' society after the peace of 1815, and as time passed it was increasingly dominated by participants in the latter conflict. In 1826, the group established itself as the Military Society of 1812, and in 1848 it merged with a similar organization, the Veterans Corps of Artillery. The ranks of living 1812 veterans thinned substantially in the second half of the 1800s, and in 1890 the organization transformed its regulations to allow admission of hereditary members.

In Baltimore, 1812 memories were more fully cultivated. Here and in other places similarly visited and indelibly marked by the war (for example, Plattsburgh, New York, Cleveland, Ohio, or New Orleans, Louisiana), public memory endured, or at least faded less dramatically. As military crisis passed after 1815, particularly in towns, cities, and regions removed from the war's theatre, the War of 1812 was barely remembered, except by those who had actually served. But not in Baltimore. The militia companies and regular troops that successfully repelled the British attack on the city in 1814 became known as the Baltimore "Defenders." They gathered on the first anniversary of the defense on September 12, 1815, to celebrate the occasion and lay the cornerstone for the city's Battle Monument. Thereafter, the commemoration became an annual event. In 1841, the Defenders established a more formal state organization, and in January of 1854, on the anniversary of the Battle of New Orleans (January 8), a national meeting of veterans at Independence Hall in Philadelphia took the first steps in establishing a larger umbrella organization. Subsequent gatherings consolidated various state groups into the General Society of the War of 1812, which persists and currently includes some 30 state associations.

In the postbellum United States, War of 1812 veterans acquired relict status, not so much because of the particular importance of the war itself, but simply because they were the oldest living American veterans. Late-1800s newspapers reported their passing, particularly as fewer and fewer remained. These ancient veterans connected Americans with a remote past, nearly to the days of the American Revolution, a time untainted by the bitterness and devastation of the recent Civil War. They offered the safety of nostalgia and symbolized a generalized American patriotism. The oldest living veteran, Hiram Cronk, succumbed at age 105 in May 1905 at his home in upstate New York. He had played a minor role in the war, serving at Sackets Harbor. His daughter explained, almost apologetically, "There were a few skirmishes, but I guess the fighting wasn't what they would call

*Veterans . . . offered the safety of nostalgia and symbolized a generalized American patriotism.*

**Baltimore saluted those who fell defending the city during the War of 1812 in a manner popular at the time—an imposing, classically inspired, memorial column.**

severe. Still he was there as a soldier, and he stayed there till the war was over." Cronk's primary accomplishment—perhaps like the United States in the war itself—was simple survival. Yet despite his humble part, Cronk's longevity and the country's patriotic desires earned him a state funeral, attended by thousands in New York and Brooklyn.

The impressive public memorializing of Private Hiram Cronk exemplified the democratization of American public memory, which began early in the 1800s and grew in the aftermath of the Civil War, as America struggled to assimilate its unprecedented losses. If Cronk was emblematic of an American Everyman, however, the hereditary organizations that emerged in the 1890s, some of which elevated descendants of the War of 1812 in particular, were elitist, not plebian. The United States Daughters of 1812 and the General Society of the War of 1812 took their place alongside the more famous Mayflower Society, the Sons and the Daughters of the American Revolution, and others, which admitted members based on blood descent and thus excluded most Americans—pointedly, recent immigrants from southern and central Europe. Actually, a diverse array of Americans could claim the honor of service to their country in the War of 1812. Irish Americans were prominent in their participation, for example, even before the great waves of immigration following the Irish Potato Famine, and American Indians served distinctively and proudly as well, among them the famed Seneca orator Red Jacket and the prominent Pequot activist and author William Apess. Occasionally, the public confronted the fact that not all of the war's veterans were white, as in January 1896 when a *New York Times* headline reported the death of Peter Peterson, an African American: "A Negro Centenarian Dead; Peterson Left His Master to Fight in the War of 1812." Peter Peterson had been born a slave in 1795 and lived in bondage in Florida and Alabama before becoming a drummer boy in the War of 1812 and later a soldier in the Mexican War. Slavery endured in the United States until the Civil War, but for Peter Peterson, unlike most African Americans, it came to an end in the War of 1812.

Facing page: Veterans of the Battle of River Raisin gathered once more in 1871. The group included Emanuel Custer, a war veteran, and his son George Armstrong Custer (back row, at center), ironically linking the Indian attack at River Raisin with Custer's death in 1876.

In the late 1800s, whether populist or elitist, the memory of the War of 1812 found new utility, expressed clearly at a meeting of the United States Daughters of 1812 in 1900. The orator of the day began with the requisite gesture to the American Revolution: "I believe I shall not exaggerate when I say that a very large portion of the people of the United States are not aware of the fact that the war of 1812 constituted the coping stone of the edifice of American

**Hiram Cronk, ca. 1905.**

Hiram Cronk belonged to an elite fraternity of sorts, a small group who not only survived bloody conflict but who outlived all their fellow comrades in arms.

Men like: Jonathan Benjamin, the last veteran of the French and Indian War; Lemuel Cook, the oldest official veteran of the American Revolution; and Owen Thomas Edgar, the final survivor of the US-Mexican War. History remembers these veterans not for battlefield exploits but because each lived long enough to become an icon. As each passed, another era seemed to end. "A time always comes," observed a *New York Times* reporter, "when the very last veterans of a war pass away." At that moment, we "relegate the cataclysm they saw with their own eyes to the bloodless abstraction of recorded history."

Cronk illustrates this inevitable reality. As a teenager, he enlisted in the New York militia that defended the shipyard at Sackets Harbor in 1814. He served perhaps 100 days. Yet when he died at the age of 105, in 1905, the West Virginia *Bluefield Daily Telegraph* anointed him as "the last link connecting the simplicity of Jefferson's day with the strenuous complexity of the present."

Thousands lined the streets of New York City as his funeral cortege, "an imposing and unusual spectacle," passed by. Police, military units, and city officials, including the mayor, joined the procession. Cronk lay in state in City Hall before burial in Brooklyn's Cypress Hill Cemetery. Another chapter closed and the War of 1812 slipped from living memory.

independence." But then he referenced more recent developments: "Those of us who have lately been thrilled with pride at the annihilation of the Spanish fleet on the morning of May 1, 1898, in Manila Bay, and by the destruction of the ships of Cervera off Santiago on July 3 of the same year should bear in mind the fact that the supremacy of the American Navy was created by the war of 1812."

In an age of rising imperialism, the US Navy would play a critical role, and the War of 1812 offered retroactively a pedigree, a set of heroes, and valued lessons. When the influential historian and naval theorist Alfred Thayer Mahan added two new volumes to his series on *The Influence of Sea Power Upon History* in 1905, *Sea Power in Relation to the War of 1812*, one reviewer asserted, "the war of 1812 was, as everyone knows, preeminently a naval war." Helping to make such a claim "common knowledge" was Theodore Roosevelt, himself the author of *The Naval War of 1812* (1882); numerous editions followed, and by 1886 it was, by regulation, required equipment on all US Navy vessels. Here and subsequently, as assistant secretary of the navy, vice president, and then president, Roosevelt argued strenuously for the creation and maintenance of a powerful navy; the United States had won on the sea in 1812, he claimed, and its navy would be critical to the country's power in the coming century—a theme echoed throughout the centenary celebrations of the war, 1912–1915, and as the Great War erupted in Europe.

If feelings of Anglophobia accompanied the post-1815 rise of American nationalism, anti-English prejudices quickly faded in the United States; and by the second half of the 1800s they were replaced by a growing Anglophilia. As the 100th anniversary of the War of 1812 approached, Americans resurrected the history of Anglo-American war, but many focused particular attention to the postwar peace. "Since the close of the war the two great English-speaking nations have been at peace," a *New York Times* feature proclaimed on June 12, 1912. Another article describing upcoming centenary celebrations in 1914 similarly emphasized not war but Anglo-American peace: "the end of the battle of Plattsburg [1814] marks the beginning of the century of peace." On an earlier visit to the battle site, it was reported, the English ambassador had been impressed by "this unusual circumstance of victors and vanquished being buried together." Townspeople in Plattsburgh had tended the graves of both sets of dead. This rite of Anglo-American reconciliation—between the Blue and the Red—seemed to parallel the North-South

*July 3, 1913, making preparations for the laying of the corner stone.*

memorial rites of reunion between the Blue and the Gray that had begun in the 1870s. These acts of reconciliation, small and large, required the cultivation of some memories at the expense of others. In both cases, the animosities and causes of "civil war," which pit Britons and former British subjects, Anglo-North Americans, and then citizens of the United States against each other, were obscured, and commonalities, common histories, and common destinies were recalled. Changing circumstances and current demands—particularly the challenges of a world war—seemed to encourage former combatants to forgive and forget.

"The war to end all war" was followed by another world war, and then by yet another major conflict in Korea. The War of 1812 further slipped Americans' minds. By the sesquicentennial year of 1962, the War of 1812 had been more thoroughly forgotten; it was a mere footnote—and who reads the footnotes? A *New York Times* writer, Brooks Atkinson, commented, "Although the War of 1812 gave us our National Anthem, the celebrations of the current sesquicentennial lack exuberance. There's a good reason. In the grumpy language of World War II, it was a colossal snafu." Atkinson acknowledged, "After a century and a half, we can feel humorous about its many follies." Perhaps in a more ironic age, the ineptitude and calamities that

**The commission that erected the memorial to Perry's Victory at Put-in-Bay during the war's centennial hoped that it would instill "the lessons of international peace by arbitration and disarmament."**

characterized the war were more easily acknowledged and the actual carnage devalued. The commemoration engaged stalwart history buffs and was a boon to boosterism in those places, like Plattsburgh or Baltimore, lucky enough to have once been sites of the war's devastation. In 1964, Plattsburgh, New York, staged its festivities during the week of July 4, even though its historic battle had occurred in September. (It was better for tourism.)

On the second Saturday in May, Essex, Connecticut, remembers the day the British destroyed more than two dozen vessels in the port notorious for its privateers in the town's annual "Burning of the Ships" parade.

Perhaps the ultimate expression of the War of 1812's trivial status and folly, conveyed with dollops of local whimsy, occurs today in coastal Connecticut, in festivals commemorating the losses of two towns, Stonington and Essex, invaded by the British in 1814. For nearly 100 years, townspeople have celebrated the Battle of Stonington, in which a British naval squadron pounded the village with 50 tons of shells, rockets, missiles, and cannonballs. Miraculously, the bombardment caused little damage or bloodshed; on August 10, the townspeople declared victory and inaugurated an annual holiday, which has lagged at times but persists to this day. The April 8, 1814, invasion of Essex, Connecticut, was more costly, resulting in a short occupation and the destruction of 28 ships. On the second Saturday of each May since 1964, Essex commemorates the "Burning of the Ships" with its "Loser's Parade" down Main Street and other festive events. The moral of the story is, perhaps, it's not whether you win or lose but how you forget the game.

As a kind of visual shorthand, artists look for creative ways to personify nation states. Great Britain's Britannia has an American equivalent in Columbia. The usually pudgy, clean-shaven John Bull might be paired with Uncle Sam, tall and lean with goatee. While the histories of these icons often take murky twists and turns, Uncle Sam may have roots in the War of 1812. Let's explore.

Columbia originated in Great Britain well before the American Revolution and retained some popularity until largely supplanted by Lady Liberty toward the end of the 1800s. Similarly, two male characters vied for iconic superiority. During the American Revolution, loyalists derisively referred to a patriot as Brother Jonathan. Johnny survived beyond the Civil War, but the tide gradually turned in favor of a new character, Uncle Sam.

Most agree that Uncle Sam acquired his familiar appearance thanks to drawings by cartoonist Thomas Nast and a World War I recruitment poster designed by James Montgomery Flagg. The name of Uncle Sam, however, presents more of a historical puzzle.

Some say that the name can be traced to Sam Wilson, a meat-packer from Troy, New York. During the War of 1812, Wilson supplied beef to the army in barrels branded with the initials "U.S." Over time, the "U.S." became synonymous with "property of Uncle Sam."

In September 1961, the US Congress threw historical caution to the wind and saluted Sam Wilson as "the progenitor of America's national symbol of Uncle Sam."

**From Indian princess to Lady Liberty to Columbia and then to Uncle Sam, the embodiment of national identity shifted from the pacified female warrior of the early 1800s to the more familiar face that recruited American soldiers and sailors for World War I.**

*Americans have largely forgotten the War of 1812, but its "Star-Spangled Banner" lives on as more than a relic...*

Another New York town found a way to promote itself, at least indirectly, through its connections with the War of 1812. No battle was fought at Troy, New York, but the city is now reckoned as the birthplace of "Uncle Sam." The personification of the US federal government, Uncle Sam, dates from the War of 1812, though few connect the two. During the conflict, one Sam Wilson of Troy, New York, supplied provisions to American troops in the northern theater, often shipping this material in barrels marked with the initials "U.S." Legend has it that a soldier asked what the "U.S. stands for" and received this reply: "Why, Uncle Sam Wilson. It is he who is feeding the army." The attribution caught on, so much so that a *Troy Post* article on September 7, 1813, reported, "This cant name for our government has got almost as common as John Bull." The rest, as they say, is history.

In the end, the most lasting contribution of the War of 1812 to American public memory has been Francis Scott Key's "The Star-Spangled Banner," which still proudly waves as the country's national anthem. After Baltimore's successful defense in 1814, Key composed a poem, "The Defence of Fort M'Henry." He later set its words to the tune of a popular English drinking song, "To Anacreon in Heaven," and its name was changed to "The Star-Spangled Banner."

The heroic air employs numerous stanzas to proclaim national survival, symbolized by the flag waving over a besieged Baltimore fort. Who can fail to recall those immortal words from the third verse celebrating American destruction of its British foes? "Their blood has wash'd out their foul footsteps' pollution. / No refuge could save the hireling and slave / From the terror of flight or the gloom of the grave." Actually, nearly everyone has forgotten these embarrassingly blood-soaked phrases, from a time when slavery still existed in the United States (but not in Britain), along with the lyrics in every verse beyond the first. Even the anthem's first verse has not fared well: "Oh, say can you see, by the danzerly light?" is a question many a schoolchild has asked, ingeniously crafting a new adjective for early morning.

"The Star-Spangled Banner" was not immediately embraced or always treated with reverence. Temperance advocates parodied it in the 1800s, for example: "Oh! Who has not seen by the dawn's early light, / Some bloated drunkard to home weakly reeling?" Foreign-language versions have been common. German and Latvian

In this draft of Francis Scott Key's poem that became "The Star-Spangled Banner," notice that he changed "through the dawn's early light" to "by the dawn's early light."

translations date to the 1860s, for example, and later, Yiddish, French, and other renditions have appeared, including a Spanish-language anthem that caused controversy amid the immigration debates of 2007. In fact, the US Bureau of Education had printed the anthem in Spanish in 1919 to cultivate among immigrants a love of their new country. Not until 1931, following some forty attempts over twenty years, did Congress finally make "The Star-Spangled Banner" officially the US national anthem. Americans have largely forgotten the War of 1812, but its "Star-Spangled Banner" lives on as more than a relic, oddly embodying America as a place of adaptation, creativity, and transformation.

*Matthew Dennis is professor of history and environmental studies at the University of Oregon and author, most recently, of* Seneca Possessed: Indians, Witchcraft, and Power in the Early American Republic (*Philadelphia: University of Pennsylvania Press, 2010*).

# The War of 1812 in Canadian Memory

By Donald E. Graves

*The War of 1812, Canadian historian Charles Stacey once remarked, is "one of those episodes in history that make everybody happy, because everybody interprets it in his own way." He then elaborated:*

> The Americans think of it as primarily a naval war in which the pride of the Mistress of the Sea was humbled by what an imprudent Englishman had called "a few fir-built frigates, manned by a handful of bastards and outlaws." Canadians think of it equally pridefully as a war of defence in which their brave fathers, side by side, turned back the massed might of the United States and saved the country from conquest. And the English are the happiest of all, because they don't even know it happened.

Stacey was absolutely correct, as perhaps no other conflict in the western world has been subject to so much confusion and so many conflicting claims—to this day. This essay was not written to resolve this controversy but to discuss Canadian memories and attitudes toward the war and how they have changed in the last two centuries.

In British North America, as Canada was known before it formally became a nation on July, 1, 1867, the effects of the war were uneven. In the maritime provinces of New Brunswick and Nova Scotia, the conflict had introduced affluent times, fuelled by increased British government expenditure and a demand for foodstuffs and raw materials. Between 1812 and 1814, Canadian privateers—who had enjoyed many successes since the beginning of the French wars in 1793—depredated the American Atlantic coastal trade. One third of all US flag vessels captured during the war were taken by Nova Scotian, New Brunswick, and Newfoundland privateers. Indeed, Halifax has good reason to remember the war fondly because when British

Canadians commemorated the centennial of the Treaty of Paris (1783) that ended the American Revolution dressed in uniforms like those worn in the War of 1812, the conflict that they equated with the origins of the Canadian nation and with resistance to foreign invasion by Americans.

troops occupied Castine, Maine, in 1814, they continued to collect the American customs duties, and when the conflict ended, these funds were used to found Dalhousie College, now Dalhousie University, in that city. In a similar fashion, Lower Canada (the modern province of Québec), which, although frequently threatened, was only invaded twice by the enemy to the south, shared in the wartime economic boom created by defence spending. In Québec, as in the Maritimes, the War of 1812 is largely remembered as a prosperous time.

In Upper Canada (now Ontario), the westernmost part of British North America, the memory of the war was markedly different. American forces invaded the province seven times, large parts of it were under enemy occupation, the provincial capital was attacked twice, and the provincial legislative buildings burned to the ground by the enemy. While the eastern part of Ontario, along the St. Lawrence River, had enjoyed a measure of wartime prosperity, much of the western portion, particularly the Niagara area, was a wasteland of burned villages, abandoned farms, and recently dug graves.

Although its wartime experience differed markedly from the other provinces of British North America, it was to be Ontario's perspective of the War of 1812 that would largely dominate Canada's national memory of the conflict. This was not only because Ontario eventually became the most populous and prosperous province in Canada but also because many of the textbooks used in English-speaking Canada were written by educators from Ontario.

The Ontario perspective was slow to develop, however, as the press in British North America in the early 1800s was tiny, and there was almost no local publishing industry. This was in contrast to the situation south of the border, where numerous histories of the war appeared, some even before the ratification of peace. It was partly to counteract the spread of American books on the conflict that in 1832 David Thompson, a wartime veteran of the British army, published a "faithful and impartial account of the late war" as he believed the minds of Canadian youth "have been endangered by the poisoned shafts of designing malevolence which have every where discharged through the country, by the many erroneous accounts" from the United States. This was the first Canadian history of the war, and it was Thompson's hope that his younger readers would "catch that patriotic flame which glowed with an unequalled resplendence in the bosoms of their fathers."

This flag, adopted after Canada achieved dominion status and self-government over internal affairs, corresponded to Egerton Ryerson's efforts to reassess the history of loyalists in America.

By the middle of the 1800s, Ontario, along with most of British North America, had evolved beyond a simple pioneer society and was entering the early stages of industrialization. Concomitant with a concern to provide better educational opportunities for future generations, a wish arose to record the deeds of the past, including those of the War of 1812. In 1855 a Toronto newspaper stressed the men and women "who could accurately inform us" of the past were "fast dying, if not already dead," and urged that steps might be taken to record the early history of the province. In the late 1860s, the provincial government initiated measures to collect eyewitness accounts from the early settlers of the province, including survivors of the war. Among those who supported this initiative was William Hamilton Merritt, who possessed a distinguished wartime career as a young cavalry officer. Merritt and others urged Egerton Ryerson, the provincial superintendent of education and a leader of the Methodist church, to undertake this task, and in 1880 Ryerson published his seminal two-volume work on *The Loyalists of America and Their Times*.

By the time Ryerson wrote, the War of 1812 had taken on a distinctly heroic sheen in Canada. One Canadian author believed the very words "Eighteen Twelve" had "the virtue of an incantation" which "pulse and vibrate through the frame, summoning from the pregnant past memories of suffering and endurance and honourable exertion." Ryerson was not much less restrained and left absolutely no doubt about who was responsible for the conflict:

*"Eighteen Twelve" had "the virtue of an incantation" which "pulse and vibrate through the frame..."*

This 1882 photo shows three Haudenosaunee veterans of the War of 1812, Sakawaraton, John Tutela, and Young Warner, who fought with their British allies. The border between the United States and the Canadas divided Haudenosaunee homelands, and divided the peoples of this Native confederation against one another.

At the darkest hour of that eventful contest, when the continent of Europe was drenched with the blood of nations, the Tyrant [Napoleon] had his feet upon their neck, and England alone stood erect, taxing her resources to the utmost and shedding her best blood for human freedom, the [Jefferson's] Democratic party in the United States—the ever-anti-British party, the pro-slavery party—the party in the United States least subordinate to law and most inimical to liberty declared war against Britain and forthwith invaded Canada.

That invasion, Ryerson firmly emphasized, was defeated by the Canadians themselves. In an allusion to Leonidas at Thermopylae, he waxed lyrical about "the Spartan bands of Canadian Loyalist volunteers" who, "aided by a few hundred English soldiers . . . repelled the Persian thousands of democratic American invaders, and maintained the virgin soil of Canada unpolluted by the foot of the plundering invader."

Ryerson set the tone for a generation of Canadian historians who generally painted a picture of an unoffending people who, summoned to arms by the tocsin of war, dropped their ploughs and grabbed their muskets to fight off the undisciplined and blue-coated republican rabble and preserve British North America for the empire. There was very little pretence about objectivity in the work of these authors—as James Hannay from New Brunswick expressed it in his 1905 history of the war:

> No doubt it will be said by some critics that in this book I have been too severe on the Americans, who invaded our country, burnt our towns, ravaged our fields, slaughtered our people and tried to place us under a foreign flag [but] I see no reason why any American of the present day should feel offended [by] an absolutely truthful narrative.

The major theme in this literature was that loyalty to the Crown and self-sacrifice had prevailed in a fight against overwhelming odds. In the Canadian mind of the 1800s, this theme was personified in Major-General Sir Isaac Brock, the British general whose heroic death at the Battle of Queenston Heights in October 1812 caused him to be termed "the saviour of Upper Canada." It also led to the construction of the most impressive Canadian memorial of the war.

Top: Laura Secord, a Canadian national hero, illustrates the complicated nature of border relationships. Her father fought for the Americans in the Revolution. But Laura married loyalist James Secord and, in 1813, warned the British of an impending American attack.

Bottom: Despite medical opinions that the wound that Brock received at the Battle of Queenston Heights killed him instantly, mythology has him utter his final command in Latin—*Surgite*, "push on."

As early as 1814, the Legislative Assembly of Upper Canada had proposed the erection of a memorial to Brock, and it was duly built and consecrated 10 years later. A Tuscan column, 135 feet high with a viewing platform, it was situated atop Queenston Heights, not far from where Brock was killed. In 1840 this memorial was blown up by anti-British agitators, but almost immediately steps were taken to erect a new and more impressive monument to the fallen hero. This took the form of a 184-foot-high column surmounted by a larger-than-life statue of the general and supported by an ornate base festooned with panoplies of arms in the style of the ancient Greeks, another of those classical allusions so beloved of Victorian society. When completed in 1856, this column was one of the highest structures in the world and a fitting tomb for Brock, whose remains are interred in its base. Placed on the brow of the Niagara escarpment overlooking the Niagara River that is the border between Canada and the United States, it can be seen for miles and towers over the surrounding countryside, including the neighbouring part of New York state. This physical dominance was deliberate for, as one modern Canadian historian has remarked, Brock's splendid memorial testified, in a most visible way (especially to Americans on the other side of the river) the veneration of Upper Canadians for the man deemed responsible for their survival; as James Hannay later wrote: "the lofty column erected to his memory informs the whole world that patriotism still lives in Canada."

In the late 1800s, other memorials were erected in Canada to mark the location of such major battles as Châteauguay, Crysler's Farm, and Lundy's Lane, but the arrival of the centennial in 1912 witnessed an outpouring of patriotic celebration in Canada. It was the high noon of the British Empire, and Canada was proud to be a prominent member of that empire. That this was so was made clear by an official of the Ontario Department of Education speaking at the 100th anniversary of the battle of Queenston in October 1912. Stressing that the ceremony was being held to pay:

> due tribute to the brave men and women who so nobly and heroically struggled to preserve for us the blessing of British liberty, and of unity with our motherland. To these men and women of firm faith, and strong heart we give gratitude and reverence today, and especially to the statesman and hero who at the foot of these heights died a hundred years ago while leading Canadian volunteers to drive back invaders

In 1859, Isaac Brock's remains came to rest within a monument topped with his statue. A plaque reminded future pilgrims to site that Brock "fell when gloriously engaging the enemies of his country."

*...the arrival of the centennial in 1912 witnessed an outpouring of patriotic celebration in Canada. It was the high noon of the British Empire and Canada was proud to be a prominent member of that empire.*

who without just cause had dared to come to Canada with the avowed purpose of forcibly taking possession of our country.

One of the largest events of the centennial was the unveiling of the monument commemorating the 1813 battle of Stoney Creek near Hamilton, Ontario. Placed midway up the Niagara escarpment, this 100-foot-high tower was officially dedicated on June 6, 1913, the 100th anniversary of the battle, in the presence of a crowd of 15,000 persons including hundreds of school children, boy scouts, girl guides, and four militia regiments. The spectators watched and cheered as, initiated by a telegraphic signal keyed by Queen Mary in Buckingham Palace, 3,500 miles away, a white veil fell from the tower, the Union Jack was mechanically raised on a hoist on its roof, as massed bands played "God Save the King," "Rule Britannia," and "The Maple Leaf Forever."

Unfortunately, not many months later, a Serbian nationalist assassinated an Austro-Hungarian archduke to begin the train of events that led to the horrors of the First World War. Canada suffered about a quarter of a million men and women killed or wounded in "the war to end all wars"—about two-thirds the number of casualties of the United States, but from a population one tenth as large. The Second World War and the Korean conflict followed, and memory of the by-now-distant War of 1812 dimmed as commemoration and memorialization were devoted to more recent conflicts.

That it did not disappear entirely is due to the creation of professional federal and provincial heritage organizations that resulted in the acquisition, restoration, and preservation of historic buildings and sites related to the conflict. For example, on the Canadian side of the 35-mile-long Niagara River, there are no fewer than two forts, a dozen or so lesser structures, and four major battlefields preserved from the war. In recent decades the advent of the hobby of historical reenactment has also kept Canadians aware of the war.

But gone is the patriotic jingoism of a century ago. Since Britain, Canada, and the United States were allies in almost all the major wars of the violent 1900s, some find it embarrassing to refer to an unhappy time when they fought against each other. This was on the mind of one speaker at the dedication of the memorial at the battlefield of Chippawa (Chippewa in the United States) held in October 2001—a month after the attack on the World Trade Center—who reminded his audience that 1814:

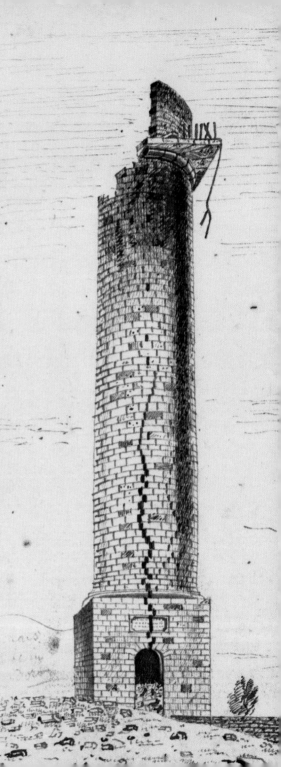

On November 8, 1861, the USS *San Jacinto* stopped the RMS *Trent*, a British mail packet, and the Union captain removed Confederate diplomats James Mason and John Slidell. In the minds of Canadians, the *Trent* Affair triggered sinister memories of border disputes and military invasions from the south. Just before Christmas in 1861, a *London Times* correspondent in Montreal reported that Canada did not intend to stand by waiting for the United States to strike again. "Armed to the teeth," Canada intended to field "fully 60,000 men in arms to resist the invasion of her soil."

President Abraham Lincoln saw the pitfalls inherent in the *Trent* Affair. "We must," he said, "stick to American principles concerning the rights of neutrals." By New Year's Day, diplomacy resolved the crisis and freed Mason and Slidell. "A feeling of relief as from some impending evil at once came over the people [of Canada]."

But the incident animated old fears. Once again, tensions between the United States and Canada/Great Britain bubbled and nearly boiled. In 1838, the Aroostook "War" stemmed from a dispute over the border with Maine. Oregon's border became a national issue in US politics in the 1840s. For decades, anti-British agitators crossed between the United States and Canada—in 1840, terrorists exploded a bomb damaging the monument of Sir Isaac Brock. And in the 1860s and 1870s, members of the Fenian Brotherhood in the United States staged raids into Canada, hoping to pressure Britain to leave Ireland.

A peaceful border, it seems, required decades of work.

**The original monument commemorating the death of General Brock became a target for anti-British agitators, and an explosion damaged the column beyond repair in 1840.**

The symbols evident at this commemoration of the Battle of Chippawa stress inclusion rather than division.

was the last year that Americans, British and Canadian soldiers fought against each other—our three nations have been firm friends and allies since that time and it is ironic that we are met here today to dedicate a memorial to a long-ago battle involving these three nations and the peace between them that has endured since that time when, as I speak, American, British and Canadian soldiers are engaged in a new conflict against a relentless and implacable foe.

A decade later, unfortunately, that conflict is still with us.

Historical anniversaries are an important part of how any nation marks its progress and defines its goals for the future. For Canada, the bicentennial of the War of 1812 will not be so much a celebration of victory (for Canadians remain convinced they won the conflict) over their neighbours as a celebration of an important milestone that ensured the independent destiny of their nation on the North American continent.

Canadian novelist and artist Douglas Coupland's 2008 irreverent sculpture in Toronto has a clear victor and vanquished; in Canada, the War of 1812 was anything but a draw.

*A well known Canadian scholar of the War of 1812, Donald E. Graves is the author or editor of six books and dozens of articles dealing with that conflict as well as ten books on other aspects of military history. He is the only non-American member of the Secretary of the Interior's Scholarly Advisory Committee on Revolutionary and War of 1812 Battlefields and the only non-British member of the Historical Advisory Committee of the Royal Armouries of Britain. He also serves as an advisor to the Minister of Canadian Heritage on the Canadian federal government's Bicentennial Commemoration of the War of 1812.*

# The Erosion of the Middle Ground: Native Peoples of the Great Lakes Region after 1815

By Doug Kiel

*Indian Country was never the same following the War of 1812. If Native aspirations were to maintain their land base and relative autonomy, then the war was most of all a loss for Native peoples throughout eastern North America.*

This is most clearly evident in the Great Lakes region. The Treaty of Ghent, which ended the War of 1812, signaled the demise of the imperial play-off system in which Native people had pitted European powers against one another to leverage the greatest advantage for themselves. For nearly two centuries, the Great Lakes region was what historian Richard White has labeled a "middle ground" between Algonquian Indians and European empires, in which both groups mutually benefited from their relationship and neither party could fully impose their will upon the other. Within this dynamic, Native peoples held equal sway in the balance of power and maintained autonomy: whites needed Indians, used them, and attempted to understand and accommodate their cultures—and vice versa. In American Indian history, 1815 marks the turning point when the middle ground gradually began to erode once the Americans assumed control of the Great Lakes region. The conclusion of the war and the eventual dissolution of the middle ground opened the door to both a US policy of Indian Removal as well as numerous Indian land cessions, two of the most apparent and disruptive legacies of the War of 1812.

Frontier settlements like Chicago, shown in 1820, continued to exist in a tangled web of land cessions, land grants to veterans, and Indian removal farther and farther to the west.

The nature of the middle ground itself changed over time. In its first phase, the middle ground was an Algonquian-French symbiosis that kept the region from erupting into violent conflict through accommodation, gift-giving, and peaceful exchange. This symbiosis endured until the

aftermath of the French and Indian War (1754–1763). In 1763 the British acquired French territory, and their newly imposed policies that rejected mediation with Indians sparked an uprising of Great Lakes tribes against British rule. Led by an Ottawa chief, Pontiac's War served as a powerful reminder to the British that their economic and military success in the region depended upon cultivating their own middle ground with the Algonquian peoples. Following the reestablishment of the middle ground and the beginning of the American Revolution a decade later, British and Indian ties grew stronger as they shared a common enemy in the Americans. In the immediate aftermath of the War of 1812, British agents and traders still exercised a great degree of influence throughout the Great Lakes region. It was nearly a decade before the British and Indian bonds were weak enough for the United States to establish dominion in the region.

The death of Tecumseh—the Shawnee leader who, along with his younger brother Tenskwatawa, assembled a multi-tribal confederacy during the War of 1812 that resisted American encroachment—marked the passing of complete Indian autonomy east of the Mississippi River. Among the Menominee Indians of Wisconsin, the respected war chief Tomah fought alongside the British to defend Mackinac Island from the Americans in 1814. Three years later, after the Americans assumed control of the region, Tomah apparently died from alcohol poisoning while in a state of depression on the island. Though some Plains tribes such as the Lakota would not reach the height of their power for decades, in the Great Lakes region the space for viable, long-term indigenous resistance to US expansion had closed by 1815. By no means, however, had the Native peoples of the region lost the power to control their own fate.

Immediately following the War of 1812, the British in Canada continued to lavish gifts on their Indian allies, which undermined the ability of the Americans to establish peace with many tribal groups, such as the Ojibwe, Menominee, Ho-Chunk, and Sauk and Fox. American officials feared an uprising led by Tenskwatawa and supported by the British, and thus the Americans occupied old British forts and began constructing many new fortifications. Dramatic American losses at the hands of British-allied Indians during the war—in the Battle of the River Raisin in southeastern Michigan and the Fort Dearborn Massacre in present-day Chicago, for example—reinforced preexisting American attitudes towards Indians. Ultimately, such fears of a new British-Indian military alliance were unfounded.

Oshawana, John Naudee, claimed to have buried Tecumseh, after his death at the Battle of the Thames, in a secret location.

The United States negotiated two treaties of Greenville, one in 1795 and another in 1814. The treaty in 1795, depicted here, allowed American expansion and trade into the Northwest Territory. Under the 1814 treaty, the government promised to "confirm and establish all the boundaries between their lands and those of the Wyandots, Delawares, Shawanoese, and Miamies, as they existed previously to the commencement of the war."

Many Native people felt that the British had abandoned them in the Treaty of Ghent, and indeed British economic interests had begun to shift from furs (a trade in which Native suppliers were central) to grain and raw materials.

Once the United States gained control of the Great Lakes region (and after their own failed attempt to preserve a peaceful middle ground), the Americans began to ignore the patterns of communication and exchange that had characterized the longstanding relationships between Indians and Europeans. Following the expulsion of the British, the Americans saw little need for military alliance with Native peoples. In the region where the middle ground had once flourished, US territories and eventually states emerged. The gradual loss of Native economic and political power after the War of 1812 meant the consolidation of American influence and a transition from an amorphous frontier to increasingly rigid borders.

European Americans were more interested in settled agriculture in the Old Northwest than they were in sustaining the fur trade that had characterized the region for more than a century. Americans aggressively pushed Indians to become virtually indistinguishable from themselves, or failing that, to relocate them from areas of American settlement altogether, a political development that came to characterize US relations in the 1800s with Indian nations westward all the way to the Pacific.

Removal was sometimes presented as a benevolent process. Lewis Cass, for example, the governor of the Michigan Territory from 1813 to 1831, believed that removing Indians to territories west of the Mississippi River would be the only means of ensuring Native American survival during a time of encroaching American settlement. Regardless of Cass' rationale, his role in negotiating the Treaty of Fort Meigs (1817) signaled the formal cession of all Indian territory in the Ohio Valley. In 1836, then US Secretary of War, Cass wrote: "the Indians now holding lands in the vicinity of Green Bay can only be considered as temporary residents there." From the perspective of individuals like Cass, the Mississippi River would become the new dividing line between Native and US settlement. Less than a century earlier, at the conclusion of the French and Indian War, the British had similarly proposed a dividing line that was as far east as the Appalachian Mountains. The Americans were focused on territorial expansion.

With the election of President Andrew Jackson in 1828, the adoption of Indian westward removal as official federal policy became an inevitability. Implementing the Indian Removal Act (1830) became one of the highest priorities of Jackson, a frontiersman from Tennessee and a famed Indian fighter who was interested in developing the region west of the Appalachians. Some tribal communities sought to avoid removal and maintain their territorial integrity by patterning their lives after Americans to demonstrate their ability to peacefully coexist and successfully adopt the "civilized" and Christian ways of their white neighbors. Jackson, however, was skeptical of Indian incorporation into American society and ultimately believed that Native people forestalled the development of the trans-Appalachian region and still posed a threat as potential allies to the British.

The Indian Removal Act authorized the negotiation of treaties that would exchange Indian lands in the east for land in the unorganized territories of the trans-Mississippi West. The prospect of removal sharply divided many

# The Erosion of the "Middle Ground"

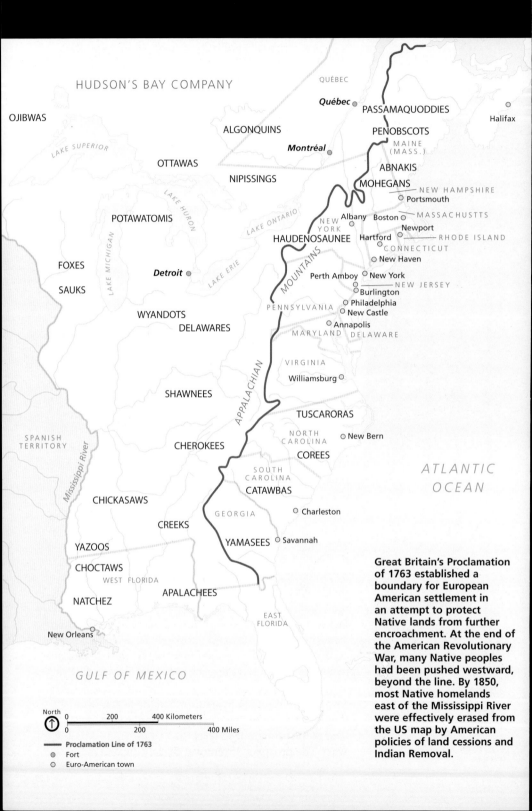

HUDSON'S BAY COMPANY

QUÉBEC

*Québec*

PASSAMAQUODDIES

Halifax

OJIBWAS

ALGONQUINS

PENOBSCOTS

MAINE
(MASS.)

*Montréal*

OTTAWAS

ABNAKIS

NIPISSINGS

MOHEGANS

NEW HAMPSHIRE

Portsmouth

POTAWATOMIS

Albany  Boston

MASSACHUSTTS

NEW
YORK

Newport

HAUDENOSAUNEE  Hartford

RHODE ISLAND

CONNECTICUT

New Haven

FOXES

*Detroit*

Perth Amboy  New York

NEW JERSEY

SAUKS

Burlington

Philadelphia

PENNSYLVANIA

New Castle

WYANDOTS

Annapolis

DELAWARES

MARYLAND  DELAWARE

VIRGINIA

Williamsburg

SHAWNEES

TUSCARORAS

SPANISH
TERRITORY

CHEROKEES

NORTH
CAROLINA

New Bern

COREES

SOUTH
CAROLINA

CATAWBAS

ATLANTIC
OCEAN

CHICKASAWS

GEORGIA

Charleston

CREEKS

YAZOOS

YAMASEES  Savannah

CHOCTAWS

WEST FLORIDA

APALACHEES

NATCHEZ

EAST
FLORIDA

New Orleans

GULF OF MEXICO

Great Britain's Proclamation
of 1763 established a
boundary for European
American settlement in
an attempt to protect
Native lands from further
encroachment. At the end of
the American Revolutionary
War, many Native peoples
had been pushed westward,
beyond the line. By 1850,
most Native homelands
east of the Mississippi River
were effectively erased from
the US map by American
policies of land cessions and
Indian Removal.

North

0    200    400 Kilometers
0         200         400 Miles

—— Proclamation Line of 1763
◦ Fort
○ Euro-American town

Native communities, with some tribal members completely opposing removal and others hoping to actively negotiate for the most favorable terms possible in light of what they believed to be an inevitable process of forced relocation. Under significant external pressure, some groups did voluntarily move west; such stories complicate the dominant historical narrative, which maintains that the United States simply swept away the vestiges of Indian communities in the East. Nonetheless, the US military and volunteer militiamen forcibly uprooted many communities that did not willingly move westward across the Mississippi River.

Within three decades of the War of 1812, the policy of Indian Removal had dramatically transformed the map of Native America and traumatized entire indigenous communities. The haunting stories of the forced removal of tens of thousands of Indians from their homelands—such as the Cherokee Trail of Tears—were in many ways a direct result of the War of 1812's outcome and the power shifts in North America. The removal policy contributed to the wide dispersal of tribal communities beyond their original homelands. For instance, forced migration partly explains why there are currently Potawatomi communities in four states: Kansas, Oklahoma, Wisconsin, and Michigan. However, Indian removal in the Great Lakes region was neither total nor inevitable. Indeed, many Native people resisted removal after the Americans gained control of the region. Many Ho-Chunks, for example, returned east to Wisconsin even after their forced relocation to Nebraska.

The era of removal was also a period of Indian land cessions. Faced with the possibility of military force,

**The symbolism included in the Great Seal of the Territory of Wisconsin reflects attitudes of the day. An Indian moves west pressured by agriculture and commerce. The motto translates as "Civilization Succeeds Barbarism."**

**As secretary of war during the Jackson administration, Lewis Cass, a veteran of the Battle of the Thames and territorial governor of Michigan, argued that Indian Removal would prevent Native peoples from being further "crushed by the onward course of events."**

*...the Mississippi River would become the new dividing line between Native and US settlement.*

many tribes throughout the Great Lakes region agreed to massive reductions of their land base. Instead of being forced westward, many Native people were banished to isolated reservations that were generally undesirable for white agricultural purposes. Native communities were often sharply divided when faced with such removal and land cession pressures. In Michigan, Wisconsin, and Minnesota, nearly all of the Ojibwe homeland—except for a handful of small reservations—had been taken through a series of treaties by 1867.

In Michigan and Indiana, "hiding in plain view" became an effective means of avoiding removal during a period of American settlement leading to state formation. In many cases, Potawatomi and Miami Indians selected from within their communities mixed-race spokespersons with European names who not only mirrored so-called "civilized" behaviors, but also looked white. By representing themselves as whites, these tribes contributed to a sense that Indians had disappeared from the landscape. In fact, often the only Native people who remained visible to whites were those impoverished individuals who had been reduced to begging.

Meanwhile, members of some Native communities had established themselves as successful farmers and traders. Magdelaine Marcot La Framboise maintained a powerful trade enterprise following the death of her husband, and her position of advantage allowed her to help her kin avoid removal. In some parts of the western Great Lakes, the landscape also aided Native persistence in the region. Numerous rivers became significant obstacles for overland travel, especially when seasonal floods created impassable

**The Battle of Bad Axe ended war with Black Hawk and the "British Band" of Indians. As with so many other frontier conflicts, it left a legacy of brutality and caused hundreds of deaths.**

barriers. Native peoples living in swamplands in northwest Indiana and southwest Michigan managed to hold their ground much longer than other tribal communities in the region. In other cases, Native people avoided removal by accommodating the federal government, establishing alliances with missionaries, and even acquiring tracts of land that served as personal reservations.

Ho-Chunk, Mesquakie, and Sauk Indians in the region bounded by the Fox, Wisconsin, Mississippi, and Rock rivers encountered new challenges and opportunities following the War of 1812, when accommodation and adaptation eventually gave way to military conflict and removal pressures. Indians in the region began trading large quantities of lead (which provided greater economic stability than fur) with Americans, who often used it in the manufacture of ammunition. Unlike most gold and silver rushes during the 1800s, in which Native people merely responded to the mining booms in their midst, Indian lead-mining success in Illinois and Wisconsin actually attracted European American settlers. The white miners, however, soon challenged Native land tenure in the region.

By the 1820s, the comparatively stable social world of the middle ground had all but crumbled in the face of a chaotic rush of European American men seeking wealth in one of the richest lead-mining regions of the world. Native people were relegated to providing services for white settlers. Later, these settlers brought their wives, and whereas Indian women in the 1700s often took French husbands as a means of facilitating intercultural accommodation, the decline of interracial marriage fostered Indian-white segregation. Tensions between Ho-Chunks and European Americans in the region ran high as thousands of miners occupied Ho-Chunk territory. In 1827, when false rumors began to spread that the Americans had handed over two Ho-Chunk prisoners to be executed by the Ojibwe, a Ho-Chunk leader named Red Bird led an uprising (known as the Winnebago Revolt) against the Americans. This brief military conflict failed to end American encroachment, but instead resulted in the Ho-Chunks being forced to cede their lands.

Five years later, the Sauk and Fox contested the validity of the Treaty of St. Louis (1804), in which four unauthorized tribal members had ceded all of their territory east of the Mississippi River. Black Hawk and his band contended that they had never signed away their lands in Illinois, and in the spring of 1832, they moved from Iowa east across the

Black Hawk, along with other Sauk and Fox leaders, was treated as a spectacle after capture following the Battle of Bad Axe. Artists painted his portrait during his imprisonment in Fort Monroe, Virginia, and crowds turned out to view the famous warrior as he was paraded through major US cities.

Mississippi River to plant corn. The Americans assumed that Black Hawk's band was hostile and quickly mobilized the Illinois militia, US troops, and Indian allies. They pursued the Sauk and Fox for months, and many of the remaining survivors were killed during the Battle of Bad Axe, as Black Hawk's band attempted to cross from Wisconsin back to the other side of the Mississippi. The nature of the Black Hawk War itself reveals how dramatically the power dynamic had changed following the War of 1812. With the exit of the British as allies, tribal groups had developed new alliances as well as rivalries. Those emerging conflicts help explain why more tribes aided the United States than Black Hawk during the conflict.

Like the tribes that had reestablished themselves in the West following removal, the Native peoples remaining in the Great Lakes region by no means became powerless victims of federal policy upon their confinement to reservations. Though the middle ground was long dead by the mid-1800s, diplomacy and compromise certainly remained alive. In both the United States and Canada, reservation-era policies aimed to diminish tribal territories and assimilate Indian individuals and communities into the mainstream white society. Native people, however, actively struggled to maintain autonomy and cultural continuity while adjusting to the new conditions of reservation life. Federal officials were often unable to implement their policies uniformly; some Native communities maintained their cultural practices and traditional subsistence economies to varying degrees, while others incorporated Native traditions into Christian practices. American and Canadian officials routinely attempted to suppress tribal leaders who resisted federal authority over Indian affairs and defended their community's territory and treaty-protected rights to hunting and fishing in their original homelands. Time and again, federal officials were forced to accommodate Indian interests, demonstrating the enduring power of Native people to influence the course of future US-Indian relations even after the middle ground had been replaced by the reservation system.

Magdelaine La Framboise's home on Mackinac Island, shown here ca. 1850, suggests the success that she had as fur trader and entrepreneur.

*Doug Kiel is a postdoctoral fellow in the Department of History at the University of Pennsylvania. He is an enrolled member of the Oneida Nation of Wisconsin and received his PhD in history at the University of Wisconsin-Madison. He studies American Indian history, federal Indian law and policy, and the history of the American West.*

# NATIONAL PARK SERVICE

## ALABAMA

HORSESHOE BEND NATIONAL MILITARY PARK
Daviston, AL
On March 27, 1814, Tennessee Major General Andrew Jackson's army of 3,300 men attacked Chief Menawa's 1,000 Red Stick Creek warriors fortified in a horseshoe-shaped bend of the Tallapoosa River. Over 800 Red Sticks died defending their homeland—never before or since in US history did so many Indians die in a single battle. The battle ended the Creek War, resulted in a land session of 23,000,000 acres to the United States, and created a national hero of Andrew Jackson.
*www.nps.gov/hobe*

## DISTRICT OF COLUMBIA

PRESIDENT'S PARK (WHITE HOUSE), Washington, DC
During the Chesapeake Campaign of 1814, the British marched on Washington, DC, and burned government buildings on August 24, including the President's House. While President James Madison inspected military preparations, his wife Dolley saved state documents and, symbolically, the portrait of George Washington before she fled. Although a fire-blackened shell remained, only the south wall and four-columned front of the north wall were saved. The Washington portrait was returned to the house, which was rebuilt and painted white, and today is known as the White House.
*www.nps.gov/whho*

## FLORIDA/MISSISSIPPI

GULF ISLANDS NATIONAL SEASHORE
Gulf Breeze, FL
British troops briefly held control of Fort Barrancas, one of three garrisons surrounding Pensacola, after Andrew Jackson led an assault on the city in November 1814. The British destroyed the fort and abandoned Pensacola, and Jackson hurried to the defense of New Orleans. Ship Island, now on the western edge of Gulf Islands, provided the British fleet with a deep-water anchorage near New Orleans. From there, Admiral Sir Alexander Cochrane gained control of the Mississippi Sound and set the stage for the British attack on New Orleans.
*www.nps.gov/guis*

NATCHEZ TRACE PARKWAY
Tupelo, MS
Created and used for centuries by Choctaw and Chickasaw Indians, the Old Natchez Trace, by the early 1800s, had evolved into a reliable land route between Tennessee, Mississippi, and Louisiana. General Andrew Jackson and perhaps thousands of soldiers were familiar with the trace and used it as a route of march to and from battle during the War of 1812, including the successful defense of New Orleans. *www.nps.gov/natr*

## GEORGIA

CUMBERLAND ISLAND NATIONAL SEASHORE, GA
British Admiral Sir George Cockburn commandeered Dungeness, the home of the late Revolutionary War veteran Nathanael Greene, when he arrived on Cumberland Island in early 1815. Cockburn also occupied nearby St. Marys, destroying the fort at Point Peter, and recruited Colonial Marines from among the island's enslaved residents before word arrived of the Treaty of Ghent. A tabby house dating to Greene's tenure, along with the ruins of a later Dungeness, remain on the site.
*www.nps.gov/cuis*

## INDIANA
**GEORGE ROGERS CLARK NATIONAL HISTORICAL PARK, Vincennes, IN**
During the War of 1812, Fort Knox III was established on the site of the former Fort Sackville, which George Rogers Clark captured during the American Revolution. The George Rogers Clark Memorial stands at the site of both former forts today. Nearby partner sites—Fort Knox II, for example—interpret the territorial and cultural disputes associated with westward expansion, particularly in the Old Northwest Territory, and events leading up to the War of 1812 during William Henry Harrison's Tippecanoe Campaign against Tecumseh's Indian confederacy. *www.nps.gov/gero*

## LOUISIANA
**JEAN LAFITTE NATIONAL HISTORICAL PARK AND PRESERVE, CHALMETTE BATTLEFIELD AND NATIONAL CEMETERY, Chalmette, LA**
The final major battle of the War of 1812—the Battle of New Orleans—took place on January 8, 1815, at Chalmette Plantation, just miles east of the city. This resounding American victory soon took on symbolic meaning in the United States, interpreted as a triumph of American democracy over European aristocracy and entitlement. Americans took pride in the victory and for decades celebrated January 8 as a national holiday. General Andrew Jackson became a national hero for his actions, and this renown helped win him the presidency in 1828. *www.nps.gov/jela*

## MARYLAND AND VIRGINIA
**FORT MCHENRY NATIONAL MONUMENT AND HISTORIC SHRINE, Baltimore, MD**
Fort McHenry commemorates the American defense of Baltimore during the 25-hour British bombardment in September 1814. Francis Scott Key witnessed the battle from a truce ship in Baltimore harbor and penned "The Star-Spangled Banner" upon seeing an enormous American flag hoisted over the fort the morning after the bombardment. Within days, Key's poem, set to a popular tune, spread across the nation. "The Star-Spangled Banner" became the national anthem in 1931. *www.nps.gov/fomc*

*National Capital Parks-East*
**FORT WASHINGTON PARK. Fort Washington, MD**
Fort Washington, overlooking the Potomac River, stands on the site of Fort Warburton, which was built in 1809 to guard the river approach to Washington, DC. The American garrison destroyed the fort during the British Navy's advance on the Nation's Capital in August 1814. The present fort, begun in September 1814 after the British burned the White House and other federal buildings, corrected many of the weaknesses of its predecessor. *www.nps.gov/fowa*

*National Capital Parks-East*
**OXON COVE PARK/OXON HILL FARM, Oxon Hill, MD**
In August 1814 after the fall of Fort Warburton just south of the US capital, a Royal Navy squadron advanced on the prosperous city of Alexandria, Virginia. Dr. Samuel DeButts and his family fled Mount Welby, their 205-acre plantation, as the British ships laid siege to the city just across the Potomac River. After the attack, Mary Welby DeButts wrote to her sister, telling of three Congreve rockets that landed at Mount Welby (now part of Oxon Hill Farm) during the British assault on the Washington area. *www.nps.gov/oxhi*

# Related Sites

STAR-SPANGLED BANNER NATIONAL HISTORIC TRAIL, Annapolis, MD

The Chesapeake Bay region, a center of commerce and government, became a prime target for the British during the War of 1812. The Star-Spangled Banner Trail commemorates the events and legacy of the War of 1812 in the Chesapeake and the writing of the national anthem along 560 miles of land and water routes traveled by the British and Americans. The trail connects 20 national historic landmarks, 13 NPS sites, and dozens of learning and recreation opportunities in Maryland, Virginia, and the District of Columbia.
*www.starspangledtrail.net, www.nps.gov/stsp*

## MASSACHUSETTS

ADAMS NATIONAL HISTORICAL PARK
Quincy, MA

Two American presidents, John Adams and his son John Quincy Adams, were born and raised in Quincy, just south of Boston. As vice president (1789–1797) and president (1797–1801), John Adams advocated for a larger US Navy. During his administration, the Navy launched six frigates, including USS *Constitution*, which won notable victories during the War of 1812. John Quincy Adams, who joined his father at the Old House farm after 1801, served as one of the US peace commissioners at Ghent during treaty negotiations with Great Britain in 1814. *www.nps.gov/adam*

BOSTON NATIONAL HISTORICAL PARK
Charlestown Navy Yard, Boston, MA

USS *Constitution*, perhaps the most famous US ship from the War of 1812, is berthed in the Charlestown Navy Yard. The Charlestown Navy Yard functioned as a supply and repair center for the US Navy during the war, and the battle between HMS *Shannon* and USS *Chesapeake* (June 1, 1813) occurred off Boston within sight of land.
*www.nps.gov/bost*

JOHN H. CHAFEE BLACKSTONE RIVER VALLEY NATIONAL HERITAGE CORRIDOR, Woonsocket, RI

The Embargo Act of 1807, enacted to punish British and French merchants and end attacks on neutral US ships, had unintended consequences. The embargo and the war undermined national unity and provoked protests, particularly in New England. With the supply of British textiles cut off, the number of cotton spinning mills in the Blackstone Valley jumped from eight in 1809 to 42 in 1815. Along with the new mills came mill villages—a hallmark of the valley's Industrial Revolution.
*www.nps.gov/blac*

SALEM MARITIME NATIONAL HISTORIC SITE
Salem, MA

With a long history of shipbuilding and global trade, Salem felt the impact of British trade restrictions and the impressment of American sailors—issues that helped spark the War of 1812. More than 40 privateers operated out of Salem during the War of 1812, including legendary ships like *Fame*, *Black Vomit*, and *Revenge*. Moored at the Derby Wharf on Salem's waterfront is the *Friendship*, a replica of a 1797 East Indiaman merchant sailing vessel captured by a British warship in September 1812.
*www.nps.gov/sama*

SPRINGFIELD ARMORY NATIONAL HISTORIC SITE
Springfield, MA

Springfield Armory was one of two federal factories making weapons during the War of 1812. When the onset of war focused attention on weaknesses in older model muskets, Springfield developed the Model 1812. Based on the French Charleville musket, it improved both the design and manufacturing process. Although the Springfield Model 1812 arrived too late to be of use in the War of 1812, it became standard issue for infantry and militia units.
*www.nps.gov/spar*

## MICHIGAN

**RIVER RAISIN NATIONAL BATTLEFIELD PARK**
Monroe, MI

The Battle at River Raisin, fought in January 1813, typified the conflicting interests central to the War of 1812. Tecumseh envisioned an Indian confederacy. The British wanted control of the Great Lakes and the fur trade. French habitants wanted to settle undisturbed. The Americans fought for land. It was the death of unprotected American prisoners killed after the Battle of Frenchtown, however, that provided one of the war's more emotional—and polemical—rallying cries, "Remember the Raisin." *www.nps.gov/rira*

## NEW YORK

**GATEWAY NATIONAL RECREATION AREA**
Fort Wadsworth, Staten Island, NY

Fort Wadsworth guards the Narrows at the entrance to New York Harbor. Because of this strategic location, the site has a layered history represented by fortifications that have been continually upgraded and modernized. During the War of 1812, several forts including Fort Richmond (1810), Fort Tompkins (1814), Fort Hudson (1810), and Fort Morton (1810) protected the Narrows. Though no tangible remnants of these "second system" seacoast fortifications exist today, visitors can tour several subsequent additions to the harbor's defense system. *www.nps.gov/gate*

**NATIONAL PARKS OF NEW YORK HARBOR CASTLE CLINTON NATIONAL MONUMENT**
New York, NY

Castle Clinton (known as West Battery during the War of 1812) was one piece of an ambitious defense system designed to protect the US coastline and cities like New York. The D-shaped fort complemented other fortifications around New York Harbor, particularly East Battery (Castle William on Governors Island). Completed in 1811, Castle Clinton's military origin remains obvious although it never saw combat and has, over time, served as an aquarium, opera house, and immigration station. *www.nps.gov/cacl*

**NATIONAL PARKS OF NEW YORK HARBOR GOVERNORS ISLAND NATIONAL MONUMENT**
Governors Island, NY

Governors Island lies a few hundred yards off the southern tip of Manhattan, a strategic location at the confluence of the Hudson and East rivers. Constructed on the island just before the War of 1812, Fort Jay and Castle William appeared to fill an obvious defensive need. The New York Harbor, bristling with walled defenses like those on Governors Island, dissuaded British attack. Castle William survives as the first example of a post-Revolution "second system" fortification. *www.nps.gov/gois*

**STATUE OF LIBERTY NATIONAL MONUMENT**
Liberty Island, NY

Fort Wood was part of the elaborate defensive system that successfully protected New York Harbor during the War of 1812. The 11-pointed star fort on Bedloe's Island later became the base for the Statue of Liberty. Nearby Fort Gibson had a dozen artillery embrasures, barracks, and a magazine, and served as a camp for British prisoners of war. Years later, the foundations of the fort were uncovered within the immigration gateway on Ellis Island. *www.nps.gov/stli*

## OHIO

**PERRY'S VICTORY AND INTERNATIONAL PEACE MEMORIAL**, Put-in-Bay, OH

At dawn on September 10, 1813, British and American naval squadrons clashed in a three-hour battle upon Lake Erie. Prior to engagement, Master Commandant Oliver Hazard Perry hoisted his battle flag inscribed with the words "DONT GIVE UP THE SHIP." Perry's Victory and International Peace Memorial commemorates the resounding American triumph at the Battle of Lake Erie and the peace that followed. *www.nps.gov/pevi*

# Related Sites

## PENNSYLVANIA
FRIENDSHIP HILL NATIONAL HISTORIC SITE
Point Marion, PA
Albert Gallatin, secretary of the treasury during the War of 1812, built his frontier home, Friendship Hill, in western Pennsylvania. In addition to his cabinet position, Gallatin played a major role in the peace negotiations that led to the Treaty of Ghent (Belgium) that ended the war. Although many disagreed, Gallatin believed that the war "renewed and reinstated the national feeling and character which the Revolution had given and which were daily lessening." *www.nps.gov/frhi*

## UNITED STATES VIRGIN ISLANDS
VIRGIN ISLANDS NATIONAL PARK
St. John, US Virgin Islands
During the War of 1812, British troops seized fortifications on Hassel Island in the Charlotte Amalie harbor of St. Thomas in the Virgin Islands. The harbor served as a critical stopover for British convoys, and the defenses on Hassel Island helped protect Caribbean trade during the war. Today, the ruins of Fort Willoughby, Fort Shipley, and Cowell's Battery are among the only War of 1812 British fortifications remaining on American soil.
*www.nps.gov/viis*

## WEST VIRGINIA
HARPERS FERRY NATIONAL HISTORICAL PARK
Harpers Ferry, WV
George Washington personally recommended Harpers Ferry, at the confluence of the Potomac and Shenandoah rivers, as the site for one of only two federal armories. The armory manufactured about 10,000 weapons per year, but geared up to produce almost 30,000 arms between 1812 and 1814 to support the war effort. In 1814, many of the armory's skilled workmen marched off to fight the British as they advanced on the Nation's Capital.
*www.nps.gov/hafe*

# PARKS CANADA

## NEW BRUNSWICK
CARLETON MARTELLO TOWER NATIONAL HISTORIC SITE, Saint John, New Brunswick
Construction of the Carleton Martello Tower, with its thick masonry walls and circular shape, began during the War of 1812 and ended in 1815. Never attacked, the tower stands as a reminder of the extent of the American threat and, consequently, the British defence system. Between 1810 and 1847, the British built at least 11 Martello towers—the preferred architecture for coastal fortifications at the time—to defend North America.
*www.pc.gc.ca/eng/lhn-nhs/nb/carleton/index.aspx*

ST. ANDREWS BLOCKHOUSE NATIONAL HISTORIC SITE AND ST. ANDREWS HISTORIC DISTRICT
St. Andrews, New Brunswick
St. Andrews Historic District preserves the site of a 1700s British North American town. The port at St. Andrews played a modest role during the War of 1812 as a base for privateers. Town residents, vulnerable to attacks from the sea, raised funds to fortify the town. St. Andrews Blockhouse, one of many built in New Brunswick for the War of 1812, is the only survivor and one of the oldest blockhouses in Canada.
*www.pc.gc.ca/eng/lhn-nhs/nb/standrews/index.aspx*

## NEWFOUNDLAND

### SIGNAL HILL NATIONAL HISTORIC SITE
St. John's, Newfoundland

Signal Hill dominates the northeast end of St. John's Harbour, offering a strategic location for observation and military defence. Although not directly involved in combat during the War of 1812, Signal Hill was the site of the final battle of the Seven Years' War in North America—including a surprise attack by the French in 1762. As a lesson learned, the British maintained an artillery emplacement there to guard against an attack by the Americans.

*www.pc.gc.ca/eng/lhn-nhs/nl/signalhill/index.aspx*

## NOVA SCOTIA

### GEORGES ISLAND NATIONAL HISTORIC SITE
Halifax, Nova Scotia

Georges Island's strategic position in the middle of Halifax Harbour prompted the British to build a Martello tower there, during the War of 1812, as one part of a network of cannon batteries and defensive works. Designed to ward off naval attack, the round design and thick masonry walls made Martello towers resistant to cannon fire; their size and design required only a small garrison of 15 to 25 men.

*www.pc.gc.ca/eng/lhn-nhs/ns/georges/index.aspx*

### HALIFAX CITADEL NATIONAL HISTORIC SITE
Halifax, Nova Scotia

The current Halifax Citadel is the fourth military structure built on Citadel Hill overlooking the vitally important, deep-water port of Halifax Harbour, one of the largest natural harbours in the world. During the War of 1812, the hill served as an observation overlook as well as a gun battery that could bring plunging fire on any enemy ship that dared to enter the harbour. The Americans never tested the citadel's defences.

*www.pc.gc.ca/eng/lhn-nhs/ns/halifax/index.aspx*

### PRINCE OF WALES TOWER NATIONAL HISTORIC SITE, Halifax, Nova Scotia

Originally built in 1796–1797 to protect against French attack, the Prince of Wales Tower remained an important link in the defensive network that guarded Halifax Harbour against American attack during the War of 1812. The first of its kind in North America, the squat, round tower took advantage of the high ground of Point Pleasant to provide covering cannon fire for other harbour fortifications.

*www.pc.gc.ca/eng/lhn-nhs/ns/prince/index.aspx*

### YORK REDOUBT NATIONAL HISTORIC SITE
Halifax, Nova Scotia

Overlooking the mouth of Halifax Harbour, York Redoubt had an important role to play in the defence of Halifax. Strengthened during the War of 1812, the redoubt provided early warning against a surprise attack on the city of Halifax and one of Great Britain's most important naval stations in North America. The York Redoubt never needed to raise the alarm.

*www.pc.gc.ca/eng/lhn-nhs/ns/york/index.aspx*

## ONTARIO

### FORT GEORGE NATIONAL HISTORIC AND BATTLE-FIELD OF FORT GEORGE NATIONAL HISTORIC SITE
Niagara-on-the-Lake, Ontario

When the War of 1812 began, Fort George served as headquarters of the British Army and the British Indian Department in Upper Canada. British Major-General Isaac Brock marched from Fort George to win the Battle of Queenston Heights, where he was killed in action, on October 12, 1812. In May 1813, an American attack overwhelmed a small force of British regulars, Canadian militia, and First Nations allies defending Fort George, but by the end of 1813 the British had regained possession of the fort.

*www.pc.gc.ca/eng/lhn-nhs/on/fortgeorge/index.aspx*

# Related Sites

**FORT MALDEN NATIONAL HISTORIC SITE**
Amherstburg, Ontario
Fort Malden served as headquarters for the Right Division of the British Army in Upper Canada and a base for the British Indian Department. From Amherstburg, the British launched a successful attack on Detroit in August 1812 and actions against the Americans between January and August 1813. After the American navy defeated the British Lake Erie naval squadron, British forces retreated to Burlington Heights, burning both the dockyard and fort. The British rebuilt the fort after the war.
*www.pc.gc.ca/eng/lhn-nhs/on/malden/index.aspx*

**FORT MISSISSAUGA NATIONAL HISTORIC SITE**
Niagara-on-the-Lake, Ontario
With earthworks laid out in a star pattern and a heavily fortified tower that served as a cannon platform, Fort Mississauga strengthened British control of the Niagara River. The fort was still under construction in July 1814 when an American army advanced, following their victory at the Battle of Chippawa, but then, without naval support, retreated. At times of international tension, British regulars or Canadian militia occupied the fort, but it never saw action again.
*www.parkscanada.gc.ca*

**FORT ST. JOSEPH NATIONAL HISTORIC SITE**
St. Joseph Island, Ontario
As tensions escalated between the Americans and British, the garrison of Fort St. Joseph attacked the Americans at Fort Mackinac. Unaware that war had been declared, Mackinac surrendered without a shot fired, allowing the British to transfer from the weaker Fort St. Joseph. Still remote and relatively undisturbed, the remarkable assemblage of archeological features at Fort St. Joseph symbolizes the alliances between British and First Nation peoples and preserves features of a frontier outpost.
*www.pc.gc.ca/eng/lhn-nhs/on/stjoseph/index.aspx*

**FORT WELLINGTON NATIONAL HISTORIC SITE**
Prescott, Ontario
Constructed during the War of 1812, Fort Wellington stood along the St. Lawrence River, the only viable shipping route into Upper Canada. High earthworks surrounded by a palisade, revetments or storage buildings, and a substantial blockhouse protected the wharfs and warehouses associated with the transfer of river cargoes around the Gallop Rapids. Never attacked during the war, Fort Wellington was rebuilt in 1838, incorporating the 1813 earthworks in the current fort.
*www.pc.gc.ca/eng/lhn-nhs/on/wellington/index.aspx*

**QUEENSTON HEIGHTS NATIONAL HISTORIC SITE**
Queenston, Ontario
The first major battle of the War of 1812 took place at Queenston Heights. Assisted by their First Nations allies, the British Army and Canadian Militia defeated an invading American army on October 13, 1812. Major-General Isaac Brock died as he led an attack to regain the heights. The battle helped unify public opinion against the Americans and demonstrated British North America's fierce determination to defend Canada. Brock's Monument commemorates the general's heroism and marks the final resting place of his remains.
*www.pc.gc.ca/eng/lhn-nhs/on/queenston/index.aspx*

## QUEBEC

### BATTLE OF THE CHÂTEAUGUAY NATIONAL HISTORIC SITE, Allans Corners, Quebec

On October 26, 1813, the Battle of the Châteauguay, together with the Battle of Crysler's Farm two weeks later, ended the American campaign against Montreal. By strategically positioning outnumbered militia from Lower Canada on either side of the Châteauguay River, Lieutenant-Colonel Charles-Michel de Salaberry, a French Canadian, surprised, confused, and defeated the advancing Americans. De Salaberry's combat exploits made him a folk hero in Canada.

*www.pc.gc.ca/eng/lhn-nhs/qc/chateauguay/index.aspx*

### COTEAU-DU-LAC NATIONAL HISTORIC SITE
Coteau-du-Lac, Quebec

Coteau-du-Lac, North America's first lock canal, formed an important link between Upper and Lower Canada. In April 1813, British troops posted at this strategic point on the St. Lawrence River built a large, octagonal, wooden blockhouse and earthworks on either side of the canal. Although it never faced an attack, Coteau-du-Lac went into a state of heightened alert several times during American invasions in the fall and winter of 1813.

*www.pc.gc.ca/eng/lhn-nhs/qc/coteaudulac/index.aspx*

### FORT CHAMBLY NATIONAL HISTORIC SITE
Chambly, Quebec

During the War of 1812, Fort Chambly guarded the vulnerable invasion route along Lake Champlain and the Richelieu River. About 40 buildings east of the fort created a military complex the size of a small village. In 1814, as many as 6,000 troops assembled there for an ambitious but unsuccessful campaign to capture Plattsburgh, New York, on the western shore of Lake Champlain.

*www.pc.gc.ca/eng/lhn-nhs/qc/fortchambly/index.aspx*

### FORT LENNOX NATIONAL HISTORIC SITE AND THE BATTLE OF ÎLE-AUX-NOIX
St. Paul de l'Île-aux-Noix, Quebec

Île-aux-Noix played an important role during the War of 1812 as a shipbuilding base on the Richelieu/Lake Champlain front. Modest fortifications and cannon batteries protected the Royal Navy, located at the nearby Fort St. Jean. In a naval skirmish near Île-aux-Noix on June 3, 1813, cannon fire from British gunboats and musket fire from British troops on both banks of the river led to the capture of two American ships and British control of Lake Champlain.

*www.pc.gc.ca/eng/lhn-nhs/qc/lennox/index.aspx*

### FORTIFICATIONS OF QUÉBEC NATIONAL HISTORIC SITE, Québec, Quebec

The Fortifications of Québec have a long history of protecting the inhabitants of Canada. At the beginning of the War of 1812, Québec City was the only permanent fortress in Upper and Lower Canada. Throughout the war, troops garrisoned in the Fortifications defended the city, regarded as the last and most important defensive position in Upper Canada. Despite the fact that Québec was not attacked during the war, further fortification of the city continued for decades.

*www.pc.gc.ca/eng/lhn-nhs/qc/fortifications/index.aspx*

# Index

# Image Sources

Cover, Fort McHenry National Monument & Historic Shrine;

1 Boston National Historical Park;

2 White House Historical Association (White House Collection);

4, 6, 8 Library of Congress;

9 Bridgeman Art Library, London;

10 Alabama Dept. of Archives and History;

11 Bridgeman Art Library, London;

12 Fort McHenry National Monument & Historic Shrine;

16 The Granger Collection, New York;

19 Library of Congress;

21 Solomon Williams, Portrait of Major John Norton (Teyoninhokarawen), CWM1995096-001, Beaverbrook Collection of War Art, ©Canadian War Museum;

22, 23 Library of Congress;

24–25 The Granger Collection, New York;

27 Library of Congress;

27 National Portrait Gallery, Smithsonian Institution/ Art Resource, NY;

28 The Granger Collection, New York;

30, 32, 34–35, 37 Library of Congress;

38 National Portrait Gallery, Smithsonian Institution/ Art Resource, NY;

41 Library and Archives of Canada (1989-479-5);

42–43 Henry Howe, *Historical Collections of the Great West* (1855);

44 Indiana Historical Society;

46–47 Library of Congress;

48 Alabama Dept. of Archives and History;

48 Library of Congress;

50 Tennessee State Library and Archives, Penelope Johnson Allen Cherokee Collection, 1775–1878;

50, 51 Library of Congress;

52 Independence National Historical Park;

54 Library of Congress;

55 Independence National Historical Park;

56 The Granger Collection, New York;

58 Maryland Historical Society;

60–61 The Granger Collection, New York;

63 White House Historical Association (White House Collection);

65 The Granger Collection, New York;

67 Library of Congress;

68 Independence National Historical Park;

69, 70–71, 73 The Granger Collection, New York;

73 Library of Congress;

73 Photo by Christopher Becker, Courtesy of Naval Academy Museum;

75 Library of Congress;

77 Maryland Historical Society;

78–79, 80 Library of Congress;

83 Indiana University Digital Image Library;

85, 88 The Granger Collection, New York;

90, 92–93 Library of Congress;

94 Army Art Collection, US Army Center of Military History;

96 Library of Congress;

99 ©American Antiquarian Society;

100 State Archives of Florida;

101 Fort McHenry National Monument & Historic Shrine;

102 Library of Congress;

103 Louisiana State Museum, Loan of Gaspar Cusachs;

104–5 Library of Congress;

107 The Historic New Orleans Collection, Acc. No. 59-12-L.1;

108 Library of Congress;

111 Library of Congress;

113 Private Collection;

114 Maryland Historical Society;

115 The Granger Collection, New York;

117 Archives of Michigan;

119 Perry's Victory & International Peace Memorial;

120 Jim Salemi/The Middletown Press;

121 Library of Congress;

123 Maryland Historical Society;

125 "Gathering for the Parade, Loyalist Centennial" (X12548), Courtesy of New Brunswick Museum, Saint John, New Brunswick;

127 Library and Archives of Canada (C-085127);

128 "Laura Secord, Legendary Patriot, © Canada Post Corporation (1992);

128 Library and Archives of Canada (e010767950);

129 Library of Congress;

131 "S. E. view of Brock's Monument on Queenston Heights as it appeared May 9th: A.D. 1841," [1841] (Archives of Ontario, F 596);

132 Heather M. Cuthill;

133 Niagara Falls (Ontario) Public Library;

134 Library of Congress;

136 Library and Archives of Canada (e010797042);

138–39 Treaty of Greenville, Ohio, 1795, Chicago History Museum (ICHi-64806);

141 Wisconsin Historical Society (WHS-64629);

141–43 Library of Congress;

145 Mackinac State Historic Parks;

146 Horseshoe Bend National Military Park;

147 Fort McHenry National Monument & Historic Shrine;

150–53 Parks Canada;

158–59 Jean Lafitte National Historical Park and Preserve.

Chalmette Battlefield, Jean
Lafitte National Historical
Park and Preserve